CHEERS FOR RONALD BIBACE AND
RELATIONSHIP POWER

I have read '*Relationship Power*' and I have found the book to be of considerable interest and, moreover useful as a practical matter of living and dealing with inter-personal relationships.

Bernard J. Shapiro, Principal Emeritus, McGill University.

The book not only offers fascinating insights into the human condition but also brims with useful advice and practical examples... guided by Bibace's sharp pen, we quickly realize that men and women are not actually from different planets after all... who knew?

Robert Appel, BA (bestselling author and broascaster)

After reading Ronald Bibace's book '*Relationship Power*' I was impressed with how his words gave me enormous power both in my personal life and as a Rabbi in my marriage counseling for couples I am about to marry. The beauty of the book is it's focusing on the essentials which are found in the Jewish concepts of 'Yetzer Halov' and Yetser hara' (the good and the bad inclination). I found it most helpful and have already advised several colleagues to consider this essential reading as well.

Rabbi Bernhard Presler.

This revolutionary book is surprisingly based on only one idea. This idea is the crucial ingredient in every good relationship. How to implement this invaluable insight is the subject of this illuminating book.

Dr. Joel Klass,

(Author's Note: Dr. Klass was the very first mental health professional who in 2004, saw the potential value of this book and encouraged me to write it. I therefore thought it appropriate to include a more complete background on him.

Bio: Joel V Klass MD. A Board Certified Psychiatrist, has been a professor of psychiatry at the University of Miami School of Medicine, President of the Broward County Psychiatric Society, and chairman of the Department of Psychiatry at Hollywood Memorial Hospital. He has been a court appointed psychiatrist for the Dade, Broward, Palm Beach County Court and contributed to numerous continuing legal education programs for the Florida Bar. Dr. Klass has evaluated over 10,000 patients in his 30 year practice and was mentioned in a 10,000 questionnaire survey of fellow physicians as being the most desirable for care of a loved one)

RELATIONSHIP POWER

How to win love and increase your income, health, and happiness through the power of good relationships

RELATIONSHIP POWER

How to win love and increase your income,
health, and happiness through the
power of good relationships

By:

RONALD BIBACE

MILL CITY PRESS
MINNEAPOLIS, MN

Mill City Press, Inc.

212 3rd Avenue North, Suite 290

Minneapolis, MN 55401

612.455.2294

www.millcitypublishing.com

This is the Third Edition of *Relationship Power*

The first two editions published earlier in 2010, were published for critical comment only and not for sale.

ISBN - 978-1-936400-52-2

ISBN - 1-936400-52-9

LCCN - 2010936316

Cover Design and Typeset by Sophie Chi

Printed in the United States of America

Table of Contents

PART II-Applying the Theory

PART III-Broader Implications

Dedication

This book is dedicated to a very good friend and my companion for over three years, Dr. Irma Hoffman, a Jungian psychologist who passed away in 2007. For the last few years of her life, Dr. Hoffman was my constant companion and my mentor in conventional wisdom in the field of psychology.

Dr. Hoffman was a wonderful, warm, and very intelligent woman and one of the first graduates of Brandeis University. She was also the loving mother and grandmother of six children and eighteen grandchildren. She became a psychologist in later life.

When we first met, in September of 2003, I had not yet begun writing this book. I began in 2004 after discussing the insights I had then recently acquired before meeting Irma. She is the person who made sure that whatever I had to say took current psychological beliefs into account. She also made sure I became as fully aware of those beliefs as possible. She saw to it that I read and discussed with her a substantial number of college texts and other material on the subject of psychology. Initially, she was more than a little skeptical about my theories. Later she became convinced of the value of some of the ideas in this book and began using them herself in the treatment of her patients and encouraging me to get the book written.

This book is a tribute to her help and loving mentoring.

Ronald Bibace

Acknowledgement

Dr. Roger Bibace, a psychologist, is my first cousin and we grew up together in Alexandria, Egypt. He has been teaching psychology at Clark University in Worcester, Massachusetts for many years and is an accomplished author of psychological texts. When I was still a boy of nine and he was seventeen, he set my feet upon the path of introspection and self analysis by giving me Dale Carnegie's book *"How to Win Friends and Influence People"*. He has always been a supportive, loving cousin who believed I should write this book because I felt strongly about it.

That said I wish to make clear that Roger had nothing to do with the content of my book. He has neither previewed nor commented on what I have written. I take full responsibility for the material in the book. Any blame resulting from factual errors or incorrect assertions or conclusions contained herein is mine and mine alone. My cousin Roger is the psychologist in the family. I am merely an introspective individual engaged in a labor of love and motivated by a strong desire to help and entertain others, who decided to write a book.

Part I-The Theory

Chapter One

The Key to all good relationships

Would you like to significantly improve your relationships? You can! First, by understanding that the key element in all good relationships is making the other person feel good about herself[1], and then by gaining insight into what I call your "Beast". (We all have one). Your Beast is that emotional part of your brain which may very often be on the prowl to "feel good," even though the action taken to feel good may harm you and others. You will learn a lot more about your Beast in Chapter 6.

When you understand these things, you should be well on the way to healing your problem relationships and making your good ones even stronger. You will have the power to make life better for all involved; this includes those inside and outside of your direct relationships. The positive effects will help you win and keep love, as well as increase your ability to do well in your career, make you healthier as a result of less stress, and finally make you a happier person.

[1] For the purposes of this book the words him and her, he and she, and himself and herself, will be used interchangeably.

This book will give you the knowledge and tools to identify the power your particular beast has over you and what triggers your beast. You'll learn how to pacify your beast as well as the beast of those with whom you come in contact. You will have acquired what I refer to as "relationship power."

A bad relationship can bring out the beast in anyone. By taming your beast, your relationships will become stronger, more fulfilling, and positive. Your eyes will be opened to the possibilities of how different your life can be once your relationships are healed and maintained at a high positive level.

<u>My theory in a nutshell</u> :

The Theory is expressed in the Ronald Bibace Theory of Personality[2], *(which I also call: The Ronald Bibace Universal Theory of Human Behavior. My name is pronounced Bee-Base)*:

<u>All human behavior past survival is motivated by the desire to feel good about oneself.</u>

The Theory's application to relationships calls for the following:

- *Making the other person "feel good about him/ herself".*
- Doing that requires three things:
- *Learning <u>how</u> to make another person feel good about him/herself*
- *Learning about the obstacle of the <u>"two personalities"</u> in each of us which often prevents us from doing so*
- *Learning how <u>to overcome</u> that obstacle*

[2] Personality Theory is what psychologists call 'a general theory of behavior'. It is intended to develop a scientifically defensible model or view of human behavior.

A word of caution: There are critical differences between making a person *'feel good about him/herself'* and *'making a person feel good'* or making a person *'feel happy'*. Briefly, doing 'bad things' like overeating or drinking too much, can generally make us feel bad but can sometimes make us feel good or feel happy, but only temporarily. Doing 'good thing' makes us feel good about ourselves for a much longer time.[3]

The key to all good relationships

The key element to good relationships that you will find echoed throughout the pages of this book, is the fact that good relationships are dependent on one thing and one thing only which is:

The desire and ability in one person to make another feel good about him/herself.

Sometimes this happens naturally or with little effort. Often it requires a lot of work. It is the key element in all good relationships you now have, as most of you are very likely to discover when you do the 'self test' below.

The idea is simple, but do not let its apparent simplicity and 'obviousness' fool you. There is more to it than meets the eye. Nor is the application simple. That said it is a far easier and effective concept to understand and apply than anything else available of which I am aware. Teaching you how to understand this idea and how it works, and then guiding you to applying it in your relationships is the main goal of this book.

[3] "Good things" as defined by our peer group.

By mastering this and the principles outlined earlier you will not only substantially improve your relationships, but you will also become a much happier and more successful person.

Importance of understanding the concept of feeling good about oneself

It is very important to fully understand the critical concept of ***making another person feel good about herself.*** That concept is the key to opening the door to good relationships and must not be confused with any other concept. There are other concepts that may also be *very positive* but that are simply not the essential 'key' to good relationships. The concept of making another person 'happy' is the one most often mistaken for making another feel good about herself.

The confusion arises because in the same way that 'all right angles are angles but all angles are not right angles', all things that make a person feel good about herself will also make her happy, *but not all things that make her happy will make her feel good about herself.*

One can think of this critical concept as the right 'key' to a particular Yale lock. Yale makes locks that will allow many wrong keys to be inserted effortlessly and therefore seem right, but cannot be turned to open the lock. So it is with the concept. *It is the one key that can not only be inserted effortlessly and therefore seem right, but will also open the lock to the door of good relationships and therefore is right.*

That is because making another person feel good about herself, is:

- ❑ More than making another person happy,
- ❑ More than giving another person pleasure,
- ❑ More than providing sexual satisfaction to another.

- ❑ More than feeding another well
- ❑ More than giving another shelter
- ❑ More than entertaining others.

All of these things and other similar things can be very positive, but do not necessarily make another person feel good about herself. For example:

- ❑ One can make a beggar *happy* by giving him alms, but that does not necessarily make him feel good about himself.
- ❑ One can give a child *pleasure* by buying her a gift, but that does not necessarily make her feel good about herself.
- ❑ A hooker can supply a customer with *sexual satisfaction,* but that does not necessarily make him feel good about himself.
- ❑ A mother can *feed* her son and unhappy daughter-in-law very well, but that does not necessarily make either her son or her daughter-in-law feel good about themselves.
- ❑ The state can *provide shelter* to the homeless for free, but that does not necessarily make them feel good about themselves.
- ❑ A generous host can spend large sums of money *entertaining* guests lavishly, but that doesn't necessarily make them feel good about themselves.

The reason is that all of these potentially very positive activities may protect or 'feed' the body and its senses. Whereas making a person feel good about herself feeds the very essence of the individual and satisfies what might perhaps best be termed 'a craving of the soul'. It is even probable that the 'inner peace' sought and found by Buddha, Lao Tse, Confucius, and others was no more than the maximized inner ability to feel very good about themselves.

Buddha is the quintessential example of the man who was born into wealth and position. He had absolutely everything that ordinary men might desire, to wit: Power, fame, position, respect from others, unlimited sexual and other physical satisfaction, and yet was not satisfied until he gave up everything he had in the search for his 'Nirvana'.

That Nirvana may very well be what is described here in the form of the ultimate level of feeling good about oneself. Moreover, in Buddha's case it will have been achieved 'internally', independent of any outside person's approval or of any other kind of outside influence that could adversely impact the serenity and peace of that state of mind.

Should you believe this?

Why should you believe that I know anything about this subject? Let's see if I can show you. Why don't you take the following ten minute self test? It will help you quickly decide if I may be right. If not, you will only have wasted a few minutes of your time.

The Self-Test

Ask yourself: What should I be doing to achieve a good relationship with another person? Write down your answer. (Note: The test requires that you answer in terms of specific actions, not in generalities. Answers like *"Do unto others as they do unto you"* are correct in principle, but too vague to be practical.)

Make a list of the five people in your life with whom you have the best relationship. These can be spousal, family, social, work-related, or other.

Make a second list of the five people in your life who make you *feel the best about yourself.*

Compare the two lists. If they are identical or nearly identical (say four out of five are the same), you have your answer![4]

If your results are the same as the results of most others, you will find you have discovered the following:

Virtually all of the people who make you feel the best or most good about yourself are on your best relationship list.[5] You will also almost certainly find that nobody who consistently make you feel bad about yourself made the list. That is why this test is positive confirmation of my theory: *Because you have just discovered that the people with whom you have the best relationships are the same people who make you feel the best about yourself.*

These good feelings are the basis of any good, positive relationship. Do you give these kinds of good feelings? If not, do you know how? If you're not sure, this book will show you how.

A review of the results of those who took the test showed that many spoke of respect, understanding, and honest communication, as well as of a number of other positive attributes that should make another person feel good about him/herself. All of these factors do indeed help make another person feel good about him/herself. But those attributes alone, or the things we SHOULD DO

[4] A word about statistics, sampling and experimental design. If one is seeking a government grant or justification for committing major funds to a project it is often necessary to conform to the most rigorous scientific statistical testing, including technical aspects such as sampling and experimental design. The author's research is much more modest, simpler and unscientific. It relies on anecdotally asking random individuals their views on a particular subject. When virtually all offer either no answer or varying and differing answers, and then all or nearly all, come to the same conclusion after they do a simple test, there is enough supporting 'unscientific' evidence to proceed further.

[5] Some people erroneouosly include a close family member on their best relationship list because they feel they should and not because it's true. You may want to review your list in that light.

(the do's), will not produce a good relationship unless they are also accompanied by the absence of those things we SHOULDN'T DO (the don'ts) like don't nag, don't criticize, don't stonewall, don't ignore, and so on. Moreover constantly remembering all of these do's and don'ts is a significant burden for a memory expert, let alone the average person. It is obviously far easier to recall a single concept.

So remember, if you get nothing at all out of this book but Rule # 1, you will find it was well worth the time to read it.

RULE #1 – *To achieve a good relationship, you must make the other person feel good about him/herself.*

Chapter Two

The Importance of Good Relationships

A good relationship exists between two people when their interaction provides pleasure and satisfaction to both members of the relationship. We are all social animals, and we need to interact positively with others in order to be fulfilled. Therefore, good relationships are the key to happiness, good mental health, and financial success. Good relationships reduce stress, which can cause or contribute to physical and mental illness. Also, the better you get along with people, the more financially successful you are likely to be. In turn, there is nothing that is likely to do more for you in all areas of your life than learning to develop better relationships.

Good relationships do more than just make people happy. They can also create positive feelings and increase self-esteem. On the other hand, bad relationships create feelings of low self-esteem, sadness, loneliness, and eventually even depression, which in extreme cases can lead to suicide.

Characteristics of good relationships

- *The happiness and well being of each person is important to the other.*
- *Both persons look forward to seeing each other and enjoy spending time together.*

- *Each person is viewed by the other as contributing to his/her quality of life.*
- *The relationship rarely involves quarrels or fights. If and when they occur, they are resolved quickly, and the compromise leaves both parties feeling satisfied and as if they were treated fairly and with respect.*
- *Each person is ready and willing to do whatever they can to help the other out of any difficulty.*

Examples:

- *Your closest friends*
- *Your significant other in the case of happy couples*
- *Your favorite family member*
- *A special mentor*
- *A favorite student*
- *People in good relationships generally like or even love each other, and are sometimes **in love** with each other.*

Bad relationships

A bad relationship is one in which two people do not get along well, or even at all. Usually, neither person cares much for the other. Sometimes they actively dislike or even hate each other. Whenever they have to deal with each other, one or both of them regard the experience as unpleasant.

This isn't always the case for all the parties involved. Sometimes one or both of the participants in a relationship won't recognize that it's bad. On the surface, it seems good and few arguments occur, but when dissected and after probing deeper into the feelings that each person has about the other and how they feel about spending time together, they come to the realization that the relationship is in fact bad. The greater problem occurs when neither party in the bad relationship recognizes it for what it is and they go through their lives without dissecting or probing, leaving them unfulfilled and wondering why.

Sometimes, only one person considers the relationship bad, while the other person may be unaware of the situation and may even believe the relationship to be good.

In a bad relationship, either one or both people feel as follows:

- *They do not care for the other person's company and try to avoid it.*
- *The happiness of the other person doesn't matter to him or her. Sometimes he or she might even look forward to seeing the other person unhappy.*
- *Neither would be likely to want to help the other in any way.*
- *Bad relationships have the opposite effects of good relationships. Bad relationships can be bad for a person's mental and physical health, and may result in ulcers, depression, and perhaps even suicide or homicide. Bad relationships can cause unhappiness and/or financial ruin, and may actually shorten one's life.*

The importance of a good marital relationship

The single most important relationship that most married couples[6] have is with each other. Yet, we know that a good relationship between married couples is neither common, nor easy to achieve. The high number of divorces in this country is evidence of this.

[6] Or couples who are in a similar relationship with each other, whether or not they are married.

The latest figures show one divorce occurring for every two marriages in the United States. Divorce is the very painful final step in a bad relationship. That is why many couples, who have given up on their marriage but don't want to divorce are resigned to trying to *survive* within the marriage. Divorce is almost always highly traumatic. It also involves inescapable harming of the children. That is why it is not unusual for couples to prefer a bad marriage as the *devil they know*, to a worse divorce or *the devil they don't.*

The invisible divorce

This explains why some of those trying to survive a bad relationship live in a status known as an "invisible divorce."[7] An invisible divorce is a marriage in which the couple, although still living together under the same roof, is disconnected in many ways. Each spouse is really living a kind of single life.[8] Sometimes that decision is due to financial necessity. Sometimes it's done 'for the sake of the children'.[9]

A little personal history

The Dale Carnegie influence - In 1936, a very insightful man named Dale Carnegie wrote a book called *How to Win Friends and Influence People*[10] published by Simon and Schuster, about the importance of good relationships and how to achieve them. That book was first given to me in 1943 by my cousin Dr. Roger Bibace[11], a psychologist and a wonderful man. At

[7] A term coined by Harville Hendrix in *Getting The Love You Want*- ISBN: 0-8050-6895-3(pbk)

[8] This does not necessarily mean either partner is unfaithful.

[9] Whether or not the children are better off in a particular bad marriage than a divorce is not always clear.

[10] This book has been a perennial best seller for decades and is highly recommended to all who have not read it. *(Disclosure- I have no connection or financial interest in the sale of that book)*

[11] Dr. Roger Bibace earned a Doctorate in Psychology from Clark University and is a professor teaching there at the time of this writing.

the time, I was nine and he was seventeen. For years that book helped me better understand human relations.

My ADHD problem

I was born in 1934 with an Attention Deficit Hyperactivity Disorder (ADHD), a condition that was completely unknown at the time. It remained undiagnosed in my case until 1985, when I was over 50. The condition created in me a persistent behavior pattern of both inattention and hyperactivity. It drove my parents, family, and occasionally my school teachers to despair. Unfortunately, it sometimes led to extreme measures by my parents in an attempt to control it.

One of the very distressing effects of the undiagnosed ADHD was that everybody kept telling me that I was bad. Therefore, I grew up *feeling very badly about myself*, and I suffered from impaired relationships with virtually everyone.

The perceived 'death sentence'

My parents were both loving and caring people. They did the best they could with a hyperactive son at a time when no-one had even heard of ADHD. However, in a desperate attempt to control my "bad" behavior, they announced that they were going to "get rid of me" by abandoning me in a remote, deserted, and dangerous area of town *when I was only seven years-old*. I perceived that as a death sentence.

They actually drove me there feeling trapped in the back seat of a two-door car. I was unable to get out and run anywhere before the final destination, which was a twenty-minute drive from my house. I sat there, paralyzed with fear and screaming for forgiveness before they pretended to 'relent' and drove me back home. That incident marked me for life. I had 'learned' that my own parents could and would condemn me to death without reason. How then was I ever to trust anyone ever again?

The consequences of my ADHD problem

My relationship with my parents became much better in later life. I did well in school and in business and my hyperactivity problems, although still there, no longer overtly affected my parents. My father died in Egypt of a heart attack in October of 1960.

At the time, I was living in Montreal and had not seen him since 1956. I took great joy in having made my father very proud of my scholastic and business success. I was at my uncle's house (his brother) when the news of his passing came. I recall how my grandmother (his mother), my uncle, my aunt, and other relatives cried. I did not. I stood in the basement looking out of the window at the cold Montreal night and wondered what was wrong with me. I was not crying and did not seem to feel any grief.

It was only many, many years later that I finally understood how the deep-rooted reaction to that infamous trip on a perceived death sentence had somehow made it impossible for me to grieve his death. When I finally understood how I had been affected I had occasion to speak to my mother about it.

I explained how that one incident had adversely affected my entire existence. How I could never fully trust anyone, including the women I fell in love with, or the business partners I had, or even my own judgment on important business matters.

My poor mother sobbed and begged forgiveness. She told me what I knew already - that all they were trying to do was scare me a little and that she and my father never would have done it if she had realized what effect it might have on me. I told her I understood, and of course I said I forgave her.

Many months later she said to me, "You say you forgave me, but in your heart you haven't done that." I knew she was right. The rational mind within me had indeed forgiven her. The emotional Beast[12] within me had not and wasn't able to for decades more.

My mother lived in Paris, France, and she eventually had to move to an assisted living facility there. I lived in Florida, but I travelled regularly to Paris to see her and called her often. I loved her and supported her financially. She died in Paris at 90, suffering from Alzheimer's. For years prior to her passing she didn't know who I was. Even then, I still could not grieve for her.

This is one sad example of how severely bad relationships can impact a person's life. Even a single very traumatic incident can scar a person's psyche and make it virtually impossible to overcome the consequences for decades or perhaps even for life.

As a result of my feelings and to avoid being ordered around by anyone, I wanted to acquire enough money as quickly as possible so I would never have to work for others or be under anyone else's "control".

That feeling also created an aversion to reasonable business risks, which resulted in my career being substantially hampered. It also created in me a major aversion to accepting the fact that I could make mistakes. That is why I tried to arrange my affairs so that I could interpret my own actions as being right, regardless of the outcome. That is also how I managed to always do my best to feel good about myself.

[12] See complete explanation of the Beast within us all later.

Starting my own business at 22 years old.

One example of this was my decision to start my own real estate brokerage business in 1957. I had graduated in Montreal from McGill University with a Bachelor of Commerce degree in June of 1956. (It is the equivalent of a Business Administration degree in the United States). I worked part time for my uncle Joseph Pardo, in real estate, while going to school from July 1954 to the end of 1956.

I then had to decide on a career, or more specifically, self-employment or employment by others. I had barely enough savings to last nine months and I had to choose between opening my own real estate brokerage office (out of my home), or seeking employment.

Becoming rich had been my goal, since I grew up believing the only person I could count on was me. In order to try to become rich, I decided to read about all the men who had done so starting from nothing. What I found was that most of those men started their own businesses when they were still young, and most failed in their first try.

However, it was what they learned in that first try that eventually allowed them to succeed beyond their wildest dreams. That is why I decided that I would open my own business, expecting to fail and to use that failure as a stepping stone to future glory. I had thus set myself up with a win/win situation. But as it happened, I failed to fail.

Fortunately, and in spite of my ADHD, through a combination of some talent and a great deal of luck, I did succeed in working only for myself for all of my life. I started my own real estate brokerage business in 1957 when I was twenty-two years-old, and I've managed reasonably well, either working alone or with partners, for over half a century. My childhood fears motivated me to succeed and to develop a business style in which I would avoid making mistakes at all costs.

Saved from guilt and feeling bad about myself by a rational explanation

My early success in business allowed me to have a relatively easy life. That left me feeling guilty and *badly about myself.* I was getting up late, not working very hard, and yet doing well enough on interest earned on earlier deals to retire modestly at twenty-three. Meanwhile, my peers were putting in forty hours per week of hard work in sometimes very inclement weather.

It was during this time, in 1958 that I turned to my cousin, Roger, for guidance yet again. Roger said, "*You have no reason for feeling guilty because you earned what you are enjoying. You did not win a lottery, or inherit wealth. What you have and what you enjoy you earned by your own hard work. You have every right to enjoy the fruits of your labor without feeling guilty."* God bless the man. He made me feel very good about myself by pointing out my *entitlement* to the fruits of my labor. I have never felt guilty since.

Later in life, I was told by Roger that I was saved from actually becoming a bad person by my very strong personality. He pointed out that I was able to ignore everybody's views that I was bad. In support of the strong personality idea I remember my first day of school.

My very first day of school

On my very first day of school the teacher was going around the room asking every student for their name and age. When it was my turn, I got up and said my name and that I was five years-old. The teacher said, "No you're not! You are six years-old!" To which I responded, *"You just met me and you are going to tell me how old I am? I am five and not six years-old!"* The teacher let it pass.

Later, I discovered why she had insisted on telling me I was six, not five. It seems that the school had a six-year minimum age rule for admission. My parents, desperate to get me out of the house, had pleaded with the school to allow me in at five, arguing that because I was very tall for my age I could pass for six.

What Dale Carnegie's book could not do for me

Now that you know a little about my upbringing and strong personality, you can more readily understand why I read and reread Dale Carnegie's book and tried to apply his principles to my life as best I could. I found it very useful both in my social life and in business. However, for years and years I kept thinking, saying, and doing things in spite of myself that I knew were wrong. Dale Carnegie's book told me what I should be doing, but his book did not explain how to overcome my inability to do it.

My 'automatic' mental putdown of complete strangers

I specifically remember standing on a busy street in Montreal some fifty years ago waiting for a friend and watching people go by. The thoughts in my mind were constantly evoking something derogatory or unfavorable about every single person that passed me. I remember thinking, *why on earth am I looking for some flaw in everybody I see, people I don't know, will never meet, nor indeed am likely to ever see again?*

Several years passed before I understood that what I was doing was trying to subconsciously ***feel good about myself*** by mentally 'putting others down' by comparing everybody unfavorably to me.

My frustration with the "perfect man"

On another occasion, at around the same time, I recall meeting with a friend's boss. The man seemed to have everything going for him. He was charming, modest, tall, athletic, very good looking and bright, a good dresser, and the head of a major corporation. I remember saying to him in a semi-jocular manner,

"I find you a very frustrating person to be with. You are perfect. I have been looking for some flaw in you, but cannot find any. That makes me feel inferior". To which he had the charm to reply, "*If you think I am perfect, you are very much mistaken. Just talk to my wife, she will straighten you out!"* This guy was so good. He even found a way to make me feel good about myself by talking about himself in a disparaging manner!

My first epiphany - my realization that I was a "son-of-a-bitch"

I was about twenty-six at the time and partners in a real estate brokerage operation in Montreal with a man named Joe. One day we were talking about somebody's perception of me. Joe said, "The guy thinks you are a son-of-a-bitch!" I replied, "Why on earth would he say that of as nice a fellow as I am?" Joe said, "Because you *are* a son of a bitch!"

For the first time, I thought to myself, *if my own partner thinks I am a son of a bitch, then perhaps I am. If so, why am I that way?* That was the beginning of my self-analysis and introspective endeavors. It was also the first time I learned to believe that 'when a dozen people tell you that you are a hunchback, it is time to take another look in the mirror!'[13]

[13] The point being that if different people accuse you of the same character flaw, it is much likelier to be true than if you are accused of a number of different flaws by different people.

Being of an intellectual turn of mind, I was fascinated by my own inability to control my thoughts, and all too often my words and actions. I wanted to learn what made me tick and how to become a different type of person, not the son-of-a-bitch that I was being called. So I became a self-styled philosopher or a lover of wisdom, and therefore a seeker of knowledge.

Another epiphany

A few years ago I had another epiphany that gave me a clearer picture of my own motivations and as a result, of that of others. I then tested the theory with some two-hundred people. The results were extremely positive, and that is what inspired me to write this book.

Rule #2 – Good relationships are very important to health, happiness, and financial success in life.

Chapter Three

How to establish and maintain good relationships, the importance of the society grade, and the difference between men and women

The *Ronald Bibace Theory of Personality* defines what we all want and therefore is also the key to achieving good relationships. It states:

> ***All human behavior beyond survival seeks to make individuals feel good about themselves.***
>
> Implicit in that statement is the desire for people *to avoid feeling bad about themselves* .
>
> That is why 'The Ronald Bibace Theory of Personality' can be thought of as a two sided coin. One side of which is:
>
> ***The desire to feel good about oneself***
>
> and the other side is:
>
> ***The desire to avoid feeling bad about oneself***

Because of its apparent universal application the Bibace theory of Personality can also be referred to as The Ronald Bibace Universal Theory of Human Behavior.

In order to build strong relationships, it's important to understand that compared to making the other person in the relationship feel good about him or herself, all other goals are only secondary.

How we make ourselves feel good about ourselves

We feel good about ourselves when we do good things for ourselves and others and thereby experience a strong sense of self-worth and self-esteem. That feeling can also include a sense of 'feeling good' if it involves physical pleasure. I call that *'good source feeling good'*.

But *feeling good* can also arise from doing 'bad things'. However such feelings will not include 'feeling good about oneself'. I call that *'bad source feeling good'*.

The critical sense of self-worth and self esteem that we desire usually depends on whether or not we meet the values set by the society in which we live. It also depends on us *being aware* that we are receiving love. It does not help much if we are actually loved but do not feel it.

Let us examine the difference between a *'good source feeling good'* and a *'bad source feeling good'*.

Let us suppose we are at a family dinner at which we enjoy pleasant relations with all there. If we eat and drink moderately, the physical pleasure we receive will be in keeping with our society's values and we will both *feel good and feel good about ourselves.* That event is a 'good source' feeling good.

But what if we overeat and drink to excess, and as a result disgrace ourselves at the dinner? The excess food and drink will still provide us with short term physical pleasure and thus will make us 'feel good' temporarily. However it will never make us *feel good about ourselves.* That is why excessive food and drink is a *bad source feeling good.* Such *bad source feeling good* can never provide us with the critically important feeling good about ourselves we crave[14].

The Society grade

In school, we are graded for our work. We know what the grade is and where we need to improve based on the grade. In life, we are also graded by the standards of our society. But that grade is not given to us in writing. Indeed it is generally not given to us at all. It is an 'invisible grade'. That invisible grade plays a very important part in how we feel about ourselves, how well we do in our relationships, and often whom we marry. The grade involves things that are often politically incorrect to discuss. It is real, nevertheless, as well as very important to the sense we have of feeling, or not feeling good about ourselves

Our competitive society

We are reminded every day that we live in a very competitive society. The media is full of messages telling us to improve our lives by becoming slimmer, more athletic, better looking through nose jobs, breast enhancements, liposuction, hair transplants, etc., We are told to become better dressers, better educated, more potent sexually. We are encouraged to acquire a better skin tone, remove wrinkles, add muscle, and so on.

[14] The sad exception is the case of those who function outside society's rules like criminals and gang members. They can feel good about themselves by doing very bad things that are approved of by their 'group' or sub culture.

We have beauty contests, dance contests, and sports contests of every kind. We even have Presidential approval polls telling us on a daily basis the approval/disapproval level of our President.[15] It is the degree to which we meet these society standards that gives us our society grade. Moreover, our ethnicity, sexuality, height, weight, looks, educational levels, and social connections can, and often do, affect the way in which we are "graded" by our societies.

It is this grade that at least in part, controls the way most of us see ourselves and how we feel about ourselves. One of the most important parts of that society's grade is how well we compare to our own family's success. A son will usually compare himself to his father, a daughter to her mother.

How we are graded

The society we live in is sending a non-stop, ongoing message, which in part, goes something like this:

- *Virtue is better than sin*
- *Tall is better than short. (There are statistics that show that taller men and women actually make more money than short men and women[16].)*
- *Beautiful is better than ugly.*
- *Thin is better than fat.*
- *Educated is better than uneducated.*
- *Smart is better than stupid.*
- *Rich is better than poor.*
- *Strong is better than weak.*

[15] The Rasmussen poll gives us daily reports on Presidential approval/disapproval statistics.

[16] A 2004 study by psychologist Timothy A. Judge, Ph.D., of the University of Florida, and researcher Daniel M. Cable, Ph.D., of the University of North Carolina, found that every inch of height amounts to a salary increase of about $789 per year (the study controlled for gender, weight and age).

- *Generous is better than cheap.*
- *Kind is better than unkind.*
- *Fidelity in marriage is better than cheating.*
- *Athletic is better than couch potato.*
- *Talented is better than untalented.*
- *Thick hair is better than baldness.*
- *Humility is better than arrogance.*

The top Society Grade: the so-called 'A list'

We speak of "A" lists that include the best and most important people to be invited to important functions. We also sometimes speak of a 1 to 10 scale for judging people. The "A" list is a list of people to whom society gives an "A" ranking and to whom most of us would give a high 8 to 10 'ranking'. The list includes people who are rich, famous, celebrities, leaders in some field, and/or people who are extraordinary in some way that is valued in society.

What this means is that we are likely to feel good about ourselves if we meet the highest societal standards, but not if we fall short. If we take an extreme example, we can safely say that a good-looking, tall, athletic, and well-dressed graduate of an Ivy League school who is both professionally successful and very wealthy, has a beautiful wife and lovely children, and one who would therefore earn an "A+" societal grade is very much more likely to feel good about himself than a bowery bum who is drunk, jobless, penniless, obese, and homeless.

There are a few exceptions. Some people with a low society grade but who have grown up with a great deal of love and affection and therefore a high sense of self-esteem, can overcome the low grade society gave them. Unfortunately, there are very few of those lucky souls.

<u>*You need to know your society grade*</u>

Nobody tells you what your society grade is. That is because to do so would be bad manners, politically incorrect, and perhaps even illegal. For example, if two people are equally qualified to do a job, but the better looking, taller, better dressed one gets the job, the employer will never admit that the person with a higher grade got the job due to his or her looks. To do so might bring on a lawsuit for discrimination.

Even in our social life we teach children not to say anything about a person's weight, looks or demeanor, particularly if that person is exceptionally fat or ugly or scarred or otherwise suffering from some visible defect or handicap.

<u>*Be aware of the other person's society grade*</u>

We sometimes hear the adage "*clothes don't make the man.*" In real life, however, they often do. The lesson here is that we need to be conscious of the grade our society gives us and others. We need to remember that we may have to work harder to achieve the same results if society gives us a low grade.

We must also remember to lavish *more* legitimate praise and appreciation on others to whom society may also have given a low grade. But we shouldn't allow what society thinks of us to have any effect on our value as human beings. There is a significant difference in being conscious of how people see us and taking it to heart as our worth.

<u>*Your Society Grade can temporarily vary with the group in which you find yourself.*</u>

Your overall 'society grade' is generally determined by the values of the overall society in which you live. However there are times when your society grade may temporarily differ from your permanent grade.

For example a person belonging to a particular ethnic group may have a society grade that is high. That person will be treated with respect in that group as a result of that grade.

But if that person should wander into another ethnic group's 'turf' he may be viewed as an 'outsider'. That consideration may well color his entire society grade as seen by the rival group as long as he remains in that area. He may be treated as an outcast simply because of his ethnicity. In that area he is not on any A list. Rather he may be on a Z list of the most undesirable people, if such a list exists.

There are many examples in the world of such situations. Situations in which different groups share the same city, state or 'space' like a school or prison[17], and are forced by fate to live together and share power. Although they may manage to 'get along' without violence most of the time, their perceptions of each other's members will be colored by their group affiliations and so will the 'grade' they give their 'adversaries'.

French President Sarkozy's problem with being 'too short' or to be politically correct: 'height challenged'

Nicolas Sarkozy is the President of France, a Nation of some 60 million people with a long history of accomplishments. France helped the USA achieve independence from Britain in the Revolutionary War, and sired Napoleon, the greatest military leader of all time[18]. One would suppose that the societal

[17] Prisons are the best example of this. Many US prisons have very distinct groups of 'blacks', whites and 'Latinos' in which group members are protected and honored and non-members can literally be at risk for their lives.

[18] Napoleon was actually born in Corsica but is generally regarded as the greatest French and world military leader of all time.

grade this President of France sees himself as achieving is at least an A+. That should be enough to make him feel very good about himself, even though he is not particularly tall.

Not so! A news report on September 9, 2009 reported that President Sarkozy uses elevator shoes, step-up boxes behind podiums, and even allegedly chooses short people to stand beside him in photo shoots so he can appear taller. If a man like President Sarkozy can be so hung up on being a few inches shorter than he would prefer is it any wonder that the people we meet daily, who may suffer from far more serious perceived “societal deficiencies”, do not feel so good about themselves?

Brothers conflict over bankruptcy.

This is a true story about two brothers, whom I shall call Norman and Derrick (not their real names). They came to North America in 1949 as political refugees. They started a business in 1950 with a borrowed $100,000.00. The business was expected to bring in some $20,000 to $30,000 a year. However because they took some unusual and very high risks they made almost one million dollars in their very first year of business.

One million dollars in 1950, is the equivalent of between $10 million to $15 million in 2010. That much money, even split between two partners, was a fortune that assured its owner a lifetime of carefree luxury. Unfortunately, in 1951 the brothers lost almost exactly the same million dollars they had earned the year before.

There was a way out. Because the loss had occurred in a different corporation than the one that had earned the money, the brothers could allow the second corporation to go bankrupt. In which case the brothers would have no personal liability for the loss and would remain rich, while their creditors got stuck with the loss.

The idea of having their corporation go bankrupt was regarded by both brothers as a matter of great dishonor and a thing to avoid *at virtually any cost.*[19] They had to choose between staying rich, but living with the dishonor of bankrupting their company, or going broke by personally covering their corporate losses.

Faced with the same dilemma the brothers came to diametrically opposite conclusions. Derrick wanted to bankrupt the corporation, and stay rich. Norman wanted to do the 'honorable thing' and was ready to go broke to do so. The battle raged on and on and finally 'honor' won over 'greed' and the brothers gave back in 1951 all they had made in 1950.

The question is: *What caused two brothers who had been brought up together in an affluent home, both bright with potentially good futures ahead of them, see the same problem and come up with diametrically opposite solutions?*

The answer is simple: Norman had a high 'society grade'. Derrick did not. Norman was good looking, had married well and had children. Derrick was neither good looking nor happily married. There were also other "society grade" differences favoring Norman over Derrick. So Norman already felt very good about himself as a result of his society grade, while Derrick felt the opposite.

[19] Today the prevailing US attitude seems to be that bankruptcy is an acceptable alternative solution to financial problems. Many regard this as a regrettable development and an indication of the moral decline of our society.

To Norman, the dishonor of allowing the bankruptcy of a corporation he owned would make him feel *so bad about himself*, that he preferred to pay the equivalent of over $5 million in 2010 dollars, which was all the money he then had, *just to avoid that feeling.*

Derrick had very little *except his fortune* to make him feel good about himself. The size of that fortune had, in Derrick's mind, increased his 'Society Grade' dramatically. To him, giving up that fortune on a moral issue when he could legally avoid doing so would leave him broke and *feeling very bad about himself.* A feeling he regarded as being far outweighed by any potential discomfort arising from the dishonor of being involved with a bankruptcy.

That was the heart of the conflict which led to the very emotional pleading and begging by the "moral" brother Norman, that "right be done" and payment made. In the end the "moral" solution prevailed. The "moral" of the story however, is the understanding of the power that a society grade can have on the Beast within us and the minds of men.

The inferiority complex

In my first year at the University of British Columbia in Vancouver, B.C., I met a very pleasant young female student with whom I was just friends. There came a time when she opened her heart to me and said, "*You know, I am really disturbed by this inferiority complex I have.*" I asked, "*What do you mean*?"

She answered, "*Well, I am short and fat and not particularly attractive. I have no boyfriend and I am also having a lot of trouble keeping up with my school work.*" I answered her saying that she was a very charming person with a great deal of kindness and charisma, which was true. I also said that she would no doubt find a wonderful boyfriend soon enough, and that making it to college indicated that she was bright, even if she was having a little trouble with her work.

The point is that this young lady was experiencing the depressing effect of the low grade society attributed to her. I did what I could to make her feel better about herself. However, I doubt that her problem would ever totally disappear. She could perhaps control her weight, but she could not grow taller, become as beautiful as she would like, or become an A+ student.

The broker's distrustful face

One rather extraordinary incident occurred when I met a real estate broker who was interested in selling me some property. As part of his presentation, he made a point of assuring me that he was an honest man even though he knew his face made him appear dishonest. It was true that he did possess a face that did not immediately inspire confidence. What was extraordinary was that he recognized that fact and felt he needed to apologize for it.

Being conscious of the societal grade that a person believes he or she has been given allows us to become more aware of the degree of need for sincere praise that person requires.

The elitist belief

I was lucky to grow up with an elitist attitude. That improved my perception of my societal grade. It also helped compensate for my enormous lack of feeling good about myself caused by the world's reactions to my hyperactive behavior. Interestingly, my attitude was not necessarily shared by others who grew up in virtually the same circumstances. That attitude, of which I was not conscious at the time, arose from a number of things.

I was born in Alexandria, Egypt, a city founded by Alexander the Great. My family lived in the Greek Quarter, regarded as the best in the city. My father was a cotton merchant at a time and in a country where cotton was king. His offices were on Cherif Pasha, downtown, a prestigious address. We were among a favored few who belonged to the Alexandria Sporting Club, one of the finest Clubs of its kind in the world. I went to Victoria College, Alexandria, which was the finest British style public school in the Middle East. King Hussein of Jordan and other monarchs also attended Victoria College.

My class consisted of thirty students. Of these, ten were of upper class Egyptian descent, ten were of non-Egyptian descent, among them were Greeks, Armenians, Maltese, Italians, British etc., and the last ten, of which I was one, were Jewish. So I grew up thinking of myself as one of an elite group of well-off Egyptian-born Jews of European origin. My ancestors were part of the Jewish exodus from Spain to North Africa in 1492. They left when Isabella "la Catolica", Queen of Spain, decreed that all Spaniards who were not Catholic must convert, leave, or be killed.

My second class citizen status

It was only when I got to Montreal in the 1950s that I found out that Jews in North America were regarded as second-class citizens. In a conversation about the unfortunate attitude of the day by many toward blacks, my companion, a Jew himself, said, "*Remember, you are only a second-class citizen yourself!*" I was shocked. I could not believe it. But it was true.

At the time, my sister, Margie, was working for a major Canadian bank that was unaware that she was Jewish.

Six months later when they found out, they fired her. They simply said, "*We don't hire Jews.*" Interestingly enough, whether based on the evidence of disproportionate Jewish achievements in the world, or my earlier beliefs, I continue to think of myself as a Jewish elitist.

He's Jewish but he's very nice and successful

When I was in my twenties, I was dating a Catholic girl whose parents were uneducated immigrants who could still not speak English and held minimum wage jobs. Yet, because I was Jewish, they felt it necessary to apologize to their friends about their daughter's relationship with a Jew. They explained that although I was a Jew, I was very nice, very successful, and a College graduate running my own real estate business. I was amused by their attitude, but not offended by their ignorance.

To this day, I would regard the epithet of "dirty Jew" with no more anger than if somebody called me a "dirty, tall man" (I am 6'-2") or a "dirty honky." The point is that the societal grade I had was high enough that at least in that area of my life I could feel good about myself. Unfortunately, that alone was not enough to keep me from a good deal of grief.

The learning disabled

My daughter, Claudia, is learning disabled and so is her husband, Jay. Growing up, both of these young people suffered enormously. Both were the butts of continuing harassment from schoolmates, isolation in social situations, and difficulties in school work. Fortunately for both of them, they met and married, and are the happiest couple I know.

Their societal grade would not be high, however. That means they are in greater need of love and recognition for their accomplishments than might otherwise be the case. I make sure that I, for one, am (in Dale Carnegie words) *"hearty in my approbation and lavish in my praise."* The praise is sincere and well-deserved.

Claudia and Jay have each been working for a major employer for over a decade. Both receive consistent, very high employee evaluations. They are in a very good marriage and handle their finances and their home responsibilities extremely well. There is much to be praised, and I make sure I do it.

The effect of our Society Grade

The higher our society grade, the easier it is for us to feel good about ourselves. The lower our society grade, the more help we need from others to feel good about ourselves, and the more likely we are to engage in anti-social behavior. Shakespeare's Richard III opening speech '*Now is the winter of our discontent...'* attributes his murderous desire to kill his brother and become King to his deformed and ugly body, not suited to entertain the ladies in times of peace.

Another important part our society grade is how we compare with our parents.

Conditional and unconditional love

Sometimes the love we receive is unconditional. That is the best kind, and happens most often between parent and child. Sometimes the love is conditional on acceptable behavior, in which case it is less reliable. It is also sometimes unintentionally unexpressed or withheld as a result of a handicap such as ADHD (Attention Deficit Hyperactivity Disorder) by the recipient.

I was an undiagnosed ADHD child at a time when nobody knew what that was. I was rambunctious, noisy, overly talkative, and generally undisciplined. My parents and extended family found it necessary to scold and punish me often for what seemed to me no reason at all. In that situation, which lasted until I went to college at eighteen years of age, I did not feel much love. As a further result, other problems developed that took me decades to overcome.

Intellectually, of course, I realize my family loved me. But at the time, I felt little or no love from my parents and most of my family. The greatest exceptions were three aunts - Angele, Lillian, and Eddie; my cousin Roger; and later my sister Margie and my cousin Maryse; and our Chauffer, Mustapha Al Shoukri.

I will bring you to America

I remember as a ten-year-old telling him, "Mustapha, when I grow up, I will go to America, become a millionaire, and send for you." Twenty-five years later I did my best to fulfill my promise. I did all I could to locate him in Egypt, but unfortunately, I failed.

As children, we grow up trying to please Mommy and Daddy. If we succeed, and Mommy and Daddy acknowledge that with love and sincere appreciation, we tend to grow up with a strong sense of self-esteem. Later in life, we try to please our bosses and families. If we succeed, we stay happy and balanced. If we fail, we are less happy and perhaps may even become depressed or worse.

My father the diabetic and his 'shooting license'.

I had an exceptionally tough time "pleasing Daddy," because my Daddy was a diabetic. That gave him what Ernest Hemingway once described as a "shooting license." Hemingway defined 'a shooting license' in one of his books. The story was that of a wounded soldier in an army hospital ward who was unhappy with hospital service. Tired of calling the nurse without success, he threw a stool at a window and broke it.

The nurse immediately showed up and inquired as to the culprit. Before the thrower could confess, one of the other patients in the ward said, "*Anderson did it!*" to which the nurse replied, "*I see!*" and walked away.

Inquiring about why Anderson got away with breaking the window, the newly arrived soldier was informed, "*Anderson has a shooting license. That means he can do anything he wants because the doctors say he is not responsible for his actions*".

At our house, my father had his shooting license. He got it from his doctor who told my mother that as a diabetic, he should avoid all unnecessary stress. So arguing with him was taboo, regardless of whether he was right or wrong.

Supervising cotton mixing for export

My father's shooting license brings an incident to mind. I was in Egypt at seventeen years-old, and I was working for my father. Although only seventeen, I was left in charge of a cotton mixing operation in which the different kinds of cotton were cleaned and then mixed together, bagged loosely in jute bags, and then moved 150 feet in a corridor by native labor for export baling.

My father ordered me to double bag the cotton so none would fall out in the corridor and get dirty. I noticed that the corridor was perfectly clean, and that we were the only people using it. Moreover, proper single bagging was more than enough to stop cotton dropping in the corridor. So I started single bagging to reduce costs.

I was watching over the operation when my father showed up behind me and spoke these words in French "*You triple idiot! Supervisor of my ass! Did I not specifically tell you to double bag? What the hell are you doing?*"

My father was a very charismatic man with a great sense of humor. Frankly, I recall being very amused, and not at all distressed by his colorful language. I was also very secure in my belief that I had done the right thing. I very calmly explained that I was saving him money and that the cotton remained perfectly clean without double bagging. To which he screamed, "*Come with me and I will prove that you are wrong.*"

So we went down together to where the cotton had already been steam-pressed into export bales. He ordered an attendant to break open the bale and to start taking the bale apart to show me the dirt. Well, he looked and he looked and he looked, and he could not find a speck of dirt anywhere. At which time, exercising his rights as my father and my boss, and using his shooting license, he yelled, "*It doesn't matter that it is clean! It is a matter of principle!*"

My father used his shooting license and parental authority to avoid admitting error and avoid feeling bad about himself as a result.

My father's dilemma

Most of us have occasionally heard the following line when asking our parents for something: "*Do you realize that when I was your age…*" and then a speech would follow detailing the much harsher conditions in which the parent lived as compared to their children. I was used to hearing that line from my father whenever I asked for something he thought excessive.

Until, that is, I came up with a great line which won the day from then on. The line I used was, "*Dad, please try to understand. When you were my age, you were a nothing, just a poor kid from a poor family. Don't compare yourself to me. I AM THE SON OF ALBERT BIBACE.*"

That left him with a dilemma and a funny smile on his face. On the one hand, I was making him feel badly about himself and mildly insulting him by calling him a nothing, just a poor kid from a poor family.

On the other hand I was also telling him that his current position in life had reached such an exalted status that my own status, as his son, entitled me to much more than he had ever had. This made him feel very good about himself. He resolved that conflict in my favor. He never again gave me his "when I was your age" speech!

Differences in relationship approaches between men and women

The best selling book, *Men are from Mars, Women are from Venus* by John Gray, PhD,[20] asserts on page five of its introduction that the book is *"... a manual for loving relationships in the 1990s. It reveals how men and women differ in all areas of their lives. Not only do men and women communicate differently but they think, feel, perceive, react, respond, love, need, and appreciate differently. They almost seem to be from different planets, speaking different languages and needing different nourishment."*

Strategy versus tactics

It is my view that *strategically* speaking men and women are identical. That is because both want good relationships and both also seek to achieve that goal in the same way, which is to feel good about themselves and/or to avoid feeling bad about themselves.

It is nevertheless true that *tactically* men and women may well be made to feel good about themselves in different ways. The excellent insight that Dr. Gray's book provides is in being able to read into words or actions more than what the words

[20] *Men are from Mars, Women are from Venus* by John Gray, PhD, ISBN# 0-06-016848-X (1952), published by Harper Collins in 1992.

or actions appear to say, and teaching men and women to look beyond their own natural reactions to words they hear or actions they perceive.

Dr. Gray's book on how to score points with the opposite sex

The book lists one hundred and one ways to score points with a woman and twenty-six ways to show how women can score big with men. In virtually every item on both lists, the result is to make the other person, man or woman, either feel good about him or herself or avoid feeling bad about him or herself.

For example, a man is told to hug his woman whenever he gets home, ask her about her day, practice listening and asking questions, give her quality attention,. Clearly each and every one of these actions will make her feel good about herself.

A woman is told never to say "I told you so" to her man if he makes a mistake, not to punish him if he disappoints her, not to make a big deal if he gets lost driving, to apologize when she hurts him, to be happy to see him when he gets home. Each and every one of these recommendations will either make the man feel good about himself or avoid making him feel badly about himself.

That's why it is important to recognize that differences in men and women are far less strategically fundamental than they are tactically different ways of seeking the same goal.

That goal is simply to feel good about themselves or avoid making them feel bad about themselves. It is a single, all-inclusive goal that is much easier to remember than the multiplicity of specific reactions to very specific situations.

There are some exceptions. There are some situations where doing exactly the same thing will produce precisely opposite effects on a man and a woman.

The "I'm taking the scenic route" line

Men don't like to ask for directions when they are driving a car. It's a 'macho' thing that makes them *feel bad about themselves*. Women are happy to ask. It doesn't disturb them at all.

So a man who is lost may pretend he really knows where he is going. Rather than admit he's lost or ask for directions, he may blandly announce-*"I'm taking the scenic route"*. A woman will generally do the rational thing and simply ask for directions.

In both cases the action taken will either make the person (the woman) *feel good about herself* for doing the intelligent thing, or avoid making the man *feel bad about himself* for asking for directions, which he regards as a sign of weakness and incompetence to be avoided if at all possible.

Rule #3 – For improved relationships be aware of the concept of society grade for yourself and others

Rule #4 – Both men and women want to feel good about themselves-the way to achieve that may differ between the sexes.

Chapter Four

The Ronald Bibace Theory of Personality

We have discussed the importance of good relationships in life, our need to feel good about ourselves, and how the values of our society give us a grade with which we get to live. Chapter I introduced the Ronald Bibace Theory of Personality.

At best, this new idea will not help everyone. Those least likely to benefit are those with a medical condition. Obviously, there is no advice or psychological therapy that can substitute for medication. However, even those in that situation may find the ideas useful. In this Chapter we will examine and develop this concept in detail.

General outline of what a Theory of Personality means and is intended to do.

The McGraw-Hill Dictionary of Scientific and Technical Terms (6th edition) defines Personality Theory as *"A branch of psychology concerned with developing a scientifically defensible model or view of human nature – in modern parlance, a general theory of behavior."*

The Bibace Theory of Personality asserts that all material human behavior beyond survival is intended to achieve a single goal, which is to make the individual feel good about himself and/or to avoid feeling bad about himself.[21]

Since the main goal of every human being is to try and make themselves feel good about themselves thereby increasing self-esteem, it makes sense that a person who is looking for good relationships will try to provide that feeling to others. That brings us to the step by step approach of the Relationship Power method:

Step One: The only way to achieve a good relationship is to make the other person feel good about himself.

How does one do that?

Step Two: One makes another person feel good about him or herself by recognizing, sincerely and often, by both word and deed, qualities about the other person *that are important to that person* and that are considered good things by the person's peer group and by continuing reinforcement of other positive behavior.

(The next step of avoiding behavior that will make the other person feel badly about herself should follow from the first and should happen naturally unless the Beast interferes. See below.)

Achieving this step is not always easy because each of us contains two distinct entities that can be in conflict. Coping with this problem brings us to step three.

Step Three: This Step involves acknowledging that within each of us there exists the potential for destroying good relationships, regardless of our best intentions. That is because we all have two separate, but interconnected entities,

[21] Or, failing that, to make the individual simply "feel good."

which are the limbic[22] and neo-cortex[23] brains. Hereafter the limbic brain will be referred to as the "Beast" and the neo-cortex as the "Logical Me".

We must accept that our Beast can and does take over our Logical Me, and can do so without us knowing it is happening. That is what can make us think, say, and do things that we would never logically do and we often live to regret. I'm referring to those things that can cause major and sometimes fatal difficulties in relationships.

This raises the following, very important question – *How can one overcome this problem?* We now move on to step four.

Step Four: This Step consists of what I call "the Magic Switch." It is a method by which the intelligent Logical Me succeeds in controlling the emotional Beast by providing a positive substitute of feeling good about itself for the previous negative source which triggered the Beast's behavior. I call it 'magic' because it can sometimes correct behavior instantaneously and effortlessly. Moreover it can do so on a long term and apparently permanent basis.

In the following chapters, we will look at each of these steps in detail.

[22] The limbic brain can be thought of as the emotional part of the brain. The formal definition is:
limbic brain - a system of functionally related neural structures in the brain that are involved in emotional behavior -the Free Dictionary by Farlex

[23] The neo-cortex can be thought of as the 'thinking part of the brain. The formal definition is: the largest and evolutionarily most recent portion of the cerebral cortex, composed of complex, layered tissue, the site of most of the higher brain functions. *Dictionary.com*

Rule #5 – We make people feel good about themselves by complimenting them sincerely and often on the achievements they consider important and by continual positive reinforcement behavior

Rule #6 – Everybody has an emotional Beast that may sometimes prevent them from always doing what their intelligent Logical Me thinks best.

Rule #7 – There is a method called "the magic switch," which can help us control our beast/limbic brains

Chapter Five

How we make others feel good about themselves

Though it has already been stated, it bears repeating - ***beyond survival, we are all primarily motivated to feel good about ourselves,*** which is why all good relationships are based on making people feel good about themselves.

Christopher Columbus' egg

The idea of making the other person feel good about himself sounds very simple and is like the story of Christopher Columbus' egg. Christopher Columbus asked if anyone could stand an egg on its end. Nobody could. Then he did it by boiling the egg and tapping the bottom to create a base. The solution is so obvious *after one is shown the answer* that one is often convinced that one knew it all along!

The concept of making people feel *good about themselves* involves developing or adding to someone else's self-esteem. Self-esteem is recognized as an important basis of health, confidence, happiness, and success in life.

Dale Carnegie's perennial bestseller, first published in 1936, *How to Win Friends and Influence People* emphasized what he called "the feeling of importance," which is another way of saying that a person wants to *feel good about himself.*

Advice of the experts: the do's and don'ts

To achieve good relationships experts in the field of psychology and relationships offer the following comprehensive list of suggestions of do's and don'ts:

The Do's : Be accepting, considerate, tolerant, respectful, kind, loving, forgiving, trustworthy and trusting, loyal, fair, supportive, reliable, a good listener, empathic, non-judgmental, understanding, financially and otherwise responsible, and honestly communicative.

The Don'ts: Don't blame, nag, criticize, complain, ignore, or stonewall.

The effect of the do's and don'ts

One need only look at every "do" to see that every suggestion would result in making others feel good about themselves. While the same analysis for the list of "don'ts" indicates that the suggestions to be avoided would result in avoiding making them feel bad about themselves. The experts agree that contributing to someone's self-esteem is a sure way of gaining his or her trust and love.

The problem with the experts' advice is that it is extremely difficult to follow. That is because trying to simultaneously remember over twenty do's and six or more don'ts is very difficult indeed!

On the other hand remembering the single instruction of making the other person feel good about herself will usually automatically bring to mind the appropriate combination of speaking positive do's while avoiding negative don'ts. That is obviously a much simpler and doable task.

How do we do it?

Our "society grade" goes a long way toward determining how we feel about ourselves. We do have some control over that process. We can sometimes and with much effort become more of the things our society wants us to be. We can study more and become more knowledgeable, or become slimmer if we are fat, or dress better, etc. But we can't grow taller or better looking, or increase our I.Q. Therefore, we must also look to other ways to make ourselves feel good about being uniquely us.

One of the best ways to feel good about ourselves is to create and maintain good relationships with others. To do that, we must seek to make ***others*** feel good about themselves. The process is mutual and very interesting, because to achieve ***our*** goals we must help to fulfill the same goals for ***others***. It's an ongoing cycle. We do something nice for others, they do something nice for us, and we all end up in happy, fulfilling relationships. We acknowledge each other sincerely and often, those things about the other person that matter to him or her.

The Golden Girls example

An episode of the Golden Girls sitcom of the 1990s illustrates this idea. The sitcom involves three middle aged women living together. All are attractive, but Dorothy worries about her looks, Blanche about getting old and Rose about not being very bright.

A charming "Casanova" type comes to town and romances all three at the same time, with each thinking she is the only one he wants. When they find out the truth, of course, they all reject him angrily, calling him an immoral scoundrel.

However, when reminiscing lovingly about the experience, Dorothy says, *"He made me feel beautiful."* Blanche says, *"He made me feel young."* Rose says, "He *made me feel smart!"* The point being that in spite of his outrageous behavior, every one of his victims could still think lovingly about him because he "made them feel very good about themselves" in the different but very special way that was individually important to each of them

Of course, he was merely a flatterer, skilled in using his knowledge to take advantage of women, until of course, they discovered the truth. Remember that sincerity is important to the process. Flattery is not a good thing. Insincerity will be recognized and will work against you. Do not say what you do not mean.

However dishonest and unscrupulous this 'Casanova's' actions may have been, his character validates the main point of this book, which is that if you raise someone else's self-esteem, that person will enjoy your company.

The fallacy of flattery

Some people are skilled in the art of insincerely "working a room." They are flatterers. They make it a point of remembering something of importance about each person to whom they speak. Things like their favorite sport, or their children's names, or the person's birthday. Some have assistants who keep track of this information and feed it to them before their prey enters the room.

These types work for years on their game and are able to ***appear*** interested in individuals who are flattered that the person remembered them. They will walk around addressing different individuals and saying things like, *"How's your golf game?" "How's your son, Johnny, doing at Yale?" "How did you do in the Bridge Tournament last month*?" They rarely even wait for an answer, which they hardly ever really care about. These 'flatterers' just keep circulating and 'working the room' for profit of one kind or another.

Flattery may work for their purposes, because the interaction is so limited and people may be made to feel good about themselves to think somebody important remembered something about them. There is usually little chance for the people to whom they speak to recognize what is really happening. However, this type of flattery doesn't work for people interested in good relationships that go beyond seeking some kind of limited monetary or political advantage. Anyone spending time with this type of person will soon see the charade revealed. Nobody wants to be friends with a phony. So don't say what you don't mean.

The importance of mentioning positive things often

It is not enough to give a sincere, heartfelt compliment a few times and then expect the effect to last. Nor to think: *He or she already knows how I feel. Therefore, there is no need to express it at all, or certainly not very often.*

Although a degree of conscious repetition will allow one to internalize <u>*one's own behavior*</u>, it seems that no degree of repetition can ever <u>*'internalize' a permanent feeling in another of being loved, admired and considered worthy*</u>.

That is why providing positive feedback is very important and should be practiced daily. Remember that happiness in life and in good relationships is a road you travel not a destination you reach. Think of continuing positive reinforcement in maintaining good relationships as the gas you put in your metaphoric "good relationship vehicle".

<u>*Avoiding the 'Comfort Trap - even a Rolls Royce needs gas to function.*</u>

Think of your relationship vehicle as the current status of your relationship. Your "relationship vehicle" may be as great as a Rolls Royce is a great car. But even a Rolls Royce must be filled with gas or it will eventually stop. So it is, generally, about all good relationships and most particularly about good marital relationships. The 'gas' of good relationships is continual sincere appreciation and repetition of positive behavior. To do otherwise is to be caught in the "comfort trap".

That is the trap in which you think that because things are going well in your relationship you no longer need to worry about it. Those who fall into that trap may well find themselves in divorce court. Either that or they will very likely be living with a cheating or very unhappy spouse and a foul general mood.

Making another feel bad about himself: How I made a lawyer hate me

In 1955, when I was twenty one years-old, I worked part-time with my uncle, Joseph Pardo, in Montreal, while I was attending McGill University. One day we went to see a lawyer we had never met. Anxious to get my uncle as a client, and impress him with his knowledge, this lawyer told my uncle about a new Canadian Supreme Court Case that had just been published that week.

It was a case that could have lowered my uncle's income taxes. A few days earlier, the case had been reported in the Financial Post, a national Canadian publication. However, another Supreme Court case, one that came to the opposite conclusion, had also been reported in the very same article. The article closed by saying that the legal issue had not been settled.

My Beast speaks up

I very politely brought the outcome of the article to the lawyer's attention, completely wiping out his effort to impress my uncle. I was more interested in feeling good about myself, by showing my uncle how smart I was, than in thinking about the man's efforts to impress.

In response, the lawyer babbled some nonsense about how the case he cited had more substance than the other. I did have enough sense not to point out that he was wrong again.

As we walked out, my uncle said, *"Congratulations! You are barely twenty one years-old and you have just succeeded in making yourself an enemy for life."* I was appalled, and I asked why.

To which he responded, "*Here is an experienced, well-respected lawyer trying to impress me with his knowledge of the latest developments in the law, and you, a snot-nosed twenty one year old kid destroy him by showing that his presentation has no merit at all. You made him look like a fool and feel terrible about himself, and he will neither forget nor forgive you. What you should have done is remained silent and told me the truth later."* That was one lesson that I never forgot.

Often, it's the approval of others that will boost your self-confidence the most

In 1957, I went into business on my own at the age of twenty-two as a real estate broker in Montreal. My father and mother were still living in Egypt. My father had tried very hard to discourage me from that venture. He wanted me to seek employment. He wrote a long letter to me outlining his arguments against my idea. I remember writing back and explaining my reasons, but failing to convince him.

As it happened, through a combination of some talent and a great deal of luck I managed to make what was then a great deal of money in my very first year of business. Many times more money than my father had been able to accumulate in his entire business life in Egypt.

When I told my father of my good fortune, he wrote me a four page letter that I treasured and read and reread many times before it got burnt in an office fire. I still think about it and regret its burning. The letter which made me feel almost as good about myself as making the money was chock full of compliments, awe, and amazement at my success.

It meant a great deal to me as my father died in 1960 of a heart attack. The last time I saw him was when he visited Montreal in 1956, before I went into business. My mother told me that for years after he heard of my success, and until he died, he walked on air basking in the pleasure of his son's success. That, too, made me feel very good about myself.

One person's success is another person's discomfort

My financial success did not make everybody around me happy. There were two reasons for that, *both related to how my success made people feel about themselves.*

It became clear to me after I closed on my first big real estate sale's commission in March 1957, that my success was not something in which everybody would rejoice. When I first spoke to my uncle about it, his reaction was negative. He said, "*What will my father-in-law say of a young whippersnapper like you making this much money when I am still struggling*?"

Times were tough in 1957. My uncle's business was financed by his father-in-law who was an inactive, but not totally silent partner. So my uncle's first reaction was that my success would make him look bad by comparison, in his father-in-law's eyes. *That's why he reacted to my news by feeling bad about himself.* Fortunately, the feared reaction never happened. Isaac, the father-in-law, merely commented that my success was a matter of my "getting lucky" and no reflection on anybody else.

Keep your success a secret says my uncle

The next thing my uncle said was, "*I know that half the pleasure of making a lot of money is telling people about it, but you must resist that impulse, because you will make people jealous and they will dislike you. People must forgive you for your success. So the fewer people know about it the fewer people will be jealous*"

I thought to myself, *this is crazy! Of course I'm going to tell people about my success! My first client is one of the richest men in the world. I am only twenty-two years-old. I need credibility and I want glory, and I won't get either by being silent.*

I asked him what he meant by people needing to forgive me my success. He explained, "*Those who succeed exceptionally well breed jealousy, because it makes others feel less competent and bad about themselves. However, if you are truly a nice guy, they will say, 'Yes, he is very successful. But it happened to a very nice guy.'*"

The "I just got lucky" approach

There was a man I knew in Montreal called Max who, in a very short time, had become very successful in real estate. He was a builder and admired by many. The tradesman and subcontractors he dealt with would often ask him, "*How did you manage to get so successful in such a short time?*" His answer was always, "*I just got lucky or something.*"

I remember looking at him when he gave me that line and I repeated, "*Yeah it was luck **or something,***" emphasizing the *"or something";* the "something" in question obviously being talent and not luck. He laughed and said, "*I have been using that line for years and nobody has ever picked up on the **or something** before!"*

The point was that he had been doing his best to make others who were less successful feel good about themselves by allowing them to feel that he was no smarter than they were, just 'luckier', like a man who won the lottery. Yet, he wanted to add the "or something" for those who might pick up on it as a true indication of what he meant.

Making the financial partner feel bad about himself gets me fired

In 1956, I was working for my uncle after graduating from college. I worked as an assistant to my uncle in all areas of his land development business. My uncle's business was funded by his father-in-law, Isaac, a silent partner, who only got involved with major business decisions. One weekend Isaac and Joseph made a decision to buy some land from a man called "Schreiber."

On Monday morning, I was told of the decision. I disagreed with the decision, and explained why. My reasoning persuaded my uncle to change his mind, but he neglected to tell Isaac. Two weeks later, Isaac asked Joseph about progress on the Schreiber deal. When he was told about what happened, Isaac blew his top.

Ignoring the wisdom of my position (they never bought the land) he ranted about the fact that Joseph had listened to me over him. "*Who the hell does this kid think he is*?" Isaac inquired. "*Who is the boss here? Me or that nephew of yours? Fire him at once!"* he demanded, and fire me, Joseph did!

It is truly amazing that a casual, good faith, and most appropriate disagreement with one's boss, on a decision made by him and his partner/boss, can result both in a good outcome for the business, and a bad outcome for the individual responsible. Such is the power of feeling bad about oneself. It seems that the only way Isaac could feel good about himself was to exercise his abusive power to get me fired without cause.

My uncle's need to lie to the family so he could avoid feeling bad about himself

Firing me turned out to be the best thing my uncle could have done for me. But that was not how things looked at the time. My uncle was very close to his sister, my mother. Firing me without reason placed him in a very difficult position with regard to her and my family. So he asked me to lie about being fired.

To ease the pain of being fired without cause, he gave me a bonus of several months' salary. He also asked me to tell everybody that I was not fired, but had quit in order to try my luck at becoming an independent real estate broker. He also added that he would write a long letter to my parents supporting 'my decision to quit', which he did.

At the time, my parents took the "quitting" very badly and remained very concerned. Within six months, their fears were allayed.

Mr. Obnoxious tours Europe

In November of 1957, at the age of twenty-three, after having had an extraordinary first year in business, I decided to take a grand tour of Europe. I spent thirty days visiting Geneva, Milan, Rome, Paris, and London.

In October of 1956, the Suez crisis in Egypt erupted. The cause was the nationalization of the Suez Canal by Egyptian

President Gamal Abdel Nasser. Israel, France, and Great Britain immediately went to war with Egypt.

That war resulted in a mass expulsion with a bare twenty-four hours notice, of all Egyptian-born individuals whose national origins were British or French. Many other Egyptian born Europeans also left with nothing but the clothes on their backs, a suitcase, and the equivalent of about $50 in cash.

So in November of 1957, when I visited Europe, a great many then penniless Egyptian-born people of European origin were still living in poverty, many as refugees on some kind of charitable or state dole. All were economic refugees, many of whom were originally people of considerable wealth and ability in Egypt.

My father had always spoken of the Hotel George V in Paris as the epitome of fancy living. As an indication of my new found success, I decided to book a room in Paris at that very hotel. I also booked rooms at the best hotels in each of the cities I visited.

Then I went abroad and visited my friends. Everybody already knew of my financial success, yet I made an unfortunate point of making certain nobody forgot it. I became "Mr. Obnoxious."

My ignorance of relationships

I should have been downplaying my own success and trying to console so many of my peers from Egypt who were living in worse economic circumstances that any of them had ever experienced. Instead, my Beast concentrated on making sure they knew all the details of how well I was doing, what fancy hotels I was staying at, and how enormously wealthy my very first client was.

I was unfortunately so involved with making myself feel good about myself that it never even occurred to me how bad I might be making my listeners feel about themselves in comparison.

It is only much later that I realized how badly I must have made my friends feel about themselves. Fortunately, most of them forgave my behavior and did very well in later life. They did remain my friends.

The Egyptian Major who saved the Jews

An incident that occurred during the period of the 1948 Israeli War of Independence illustrates how strong the motivation of wanting to feel good about oneself can be.

Upon the outbreak of the war, the Egyptian government immediately rounded up and placed all Jewish men between the ages of eighteen and thirty in detention camps under armed guards, including my uncle Joseph[24]. That was done on the grounds that they were potentially "dangerous" to the security of the State. The move was similar to the forcible detainment of Americans of Japanese origin in 1941 after the bombing of Pearl Harbor.

My uncle was taken to a 'detention camp' where he was 'confined' along with 2,000 other Jews. Across the street from the camp was a Palestinian refugee center occupied by 6,000 young men.

One day the guards at the camp informed my uncle and the other Jewish detainees that there was a great deal of unrest in the Palestinian camp. They added that it was very likely that the refugees, who outnumbered the Jews by three to one, would attack the camp within hours, with the intent of killing everybody there.

[24] He was older than 30 at the time, but they took him anyway.

The Jews began to prepare for battle, ripping apart metal beds for weapons, and also praying, many believing they would not survive the attack.

When the Palestinians marched en masse toward the gates of the Jewish concentration camp, they were met by an Egyptian Major, who spoke these words,

"I know your grievances and I understand your frustrations, but these Jews are under my protection as head of this camp." Pulling out his revolver, he added, *"I know I can't stop you, but if you want to kill these Jews, you will have to kill me first."*

Impressed by his bravery, the mob turned back and the lives of all the Jews were spared. The point of the story is that this Egyptian Major's sense of duty was so great that, even though his sympathies were with the Palestinians, he would rather feel good about himself doing his duty, even unto death, than allow overwhelming numbers of his fellow Arabs kill the Jews he had been ordered to protect.

The "subjective rationality" or 'perception' of extremely irrational behavior – the suicide bombers

There is incomprehension in Western minds as to how suicide bombers can be motivated to kill themselves for their cause. Westerners are taught that life is precious and that courage and bravery in the service of their country are admirable traits. But they are never taught that deliberately killing oneself for a particular cause can ever be the most desirable option.

The 911 experience and the 'Christmas' bomber

Yet, we know from recent experience in the New York 9/11 attack that there are some people to whom deliberately killing themselves for a cause is a most desirable goal. In "their world", there are circumstances in which surviving is actually less desirable than dying. That appears to be the stated purpose of one or more of the surviving terrorists involved with the 9/11 attack.

On Christmas day, December 25, 2008, a Nigerian national named Umar Farouk Abdul Mutallab, (dubbed the Christmas Bomber[25] by the press) was arrested for allegedly trying to bomb an airliner over Detroit. His father, a prosperous Nigerian Banker, had earlier alerted US authorities to the possibility of his son being a threat.

Mutallab and several of the 911 terrorists came from 'privileged' backgrounds not usually associated with sources of antisocial behavior.

Some of the captured terrorists are reported to have stated that they look forward to being condemned to death at their trial and dying for their cause. In their subjective reality, the death they seek is a very good thing. They are avowed Jihadists, apparently sincerely believing that dying for their cause will get them a direct ticket to heaven.

Acting in accordance with that belief is what makes them feel good about themselves. To them, what Western minds would regard as totally irrational is completely rational. That is 'their perception'.

It does Westerners little good to wring their hands and comment that these people are "crazy" or "fanatics" or "Jihadist murderers." It might be better to look into the *subjective reality* of what these people seek to "make themselves feel good about themselves" with a view to finding less lethal substitute behavior that might be acceptable.

[25] Also known as the underpants bomber, because that is where he hid the explosives.

A word on 'subjective' and 'objective' reality.

If a blind man, a color blind man, and a seeing man get together to speak of the world, what is their reality? The blind man sees nothing and that is his reality. The color blind man sees only the color his deficient vision can perceive and that is his reality. The seeing man sees everything 'normally,' but is limited to colors that are in the visible spectrum, which is the most that the 'unaided' human eye can see. He cannot see colors that are ultraviolet or infrared because human eyes cannot detect those colors.

So whose reality is the "true" one? The answer is that all are 'right' and all are 'wrong'. The reason is that there are two realities for each of us. The first is the *"subjective reality,"* which is limited to what we are able to perceive and therefore believe. The second is *"objective reality,"* which can never be absolutely known, but to which we can hope to get closer and closer.

For example if the normal eyed person is given 'night vision' goggles as a visual aid, his 'subjective reality' will increase. He will be closer to, but never at, *objective reality.*

Therefore, when we speak of some groups of people consistently doing things like killing innocent people by suicide bombings, we need to understand that *in their world,* or their *subjective realities,* such behavior is desirable and 'right',.

It is necessary to acknowledge that a *subjective reality* can exist in which people can believe that murdering innocent people in the name of their religion is right. Only then can we hope to first understand their *subjective reality* and then hopefully learn how to stop them.

In less extreme cases that affect us in our daily lives, we can also begin to understand how two people's subjective realities will provide each with the 'moral certainty' that each is 100% right and that the other is 100% wrong.

The pro choice and pro life 'subjective realities'

The pro-choicers : protectors of freedom for women

An excellent example of the difference in "subjective realities" is how two major groups in the USA and elsewhere look upon the right of a woman to terminate pregnancy. Each side frames the debate in a manner and in language that reflects their own subjective reality. For example those who favor a woman's right to terminate a pregnancy call themselves 'pro-choice'. Their opponents, they argue, are 'against choice'. The clear implication is that a woman in a free society should have the freedom of choice to do as she and she alone sees fit with her own body, including terminating an unwanted pregnancy. Anything less, they argue, is not freedom.

The pro-lifers: protectors of the lives of 'unborn babies'

Those who don't agree call themselves 'pro-life'. The clear implication is that their opponents are somehow *against* life. They argue that life begins at conception. Therefore terminating a pregnancy at any time constitutes "the killing of an unborn child". Some even call the doctors performing legal terminations "murderers". Others may even go to greater lengths and have been known to commit violent acts, including murder, against those they think are "killing babies". That is the ultimate irony.

One side argues for the right of a woman to choose. The other argues for the right of a 'child' to live. Neither side acknowledges the *'subjective reality'* of the other. Each side functions as if its own '*subjective reality*' is the one and only *'objective reality'.* Each side therefore remains convinced that the other side's position is either seriously 'misguided' at best or even criminally wrong at worst.

Is it then at all surprising that some people in our own daily relationships may have very strongly held opposing views on any particular subject even with the same information available to both?

The Muslim Jihadists vs the Muslim majority

It is also interesting to consider the "realities" of two different groups of Muslims referring to the same religion. To a miniscule minority of Muslim Jihadists their religion decrees that they should kill non believers in suicide bomber attacks. They do this even to certain other Muslims, whom a non Muslim could reasonably assume would be viewed as believers.

To the overwhelming majority of Muslims, such actions are a deplorable and reprehensible misinterpretation of their religion. It is amazing to see how the interpretation of the same text can and does produce diametrically opposed views on recommended action.

"Schadenfreude" or the glee we feel at the misfortune of others- Why the Beast "feels good" when the "mighty fall"

'Newsworthiness' of President Obama versus Ponzi schemer Scott Rothstein and Tiger Woods

On December 1, 2009, United States President Barack Obama made a major speech about the war in Afghanistan. This very important speech had been expected since August 2009. Obama had campaigned on a platform of ending the war as quickly as possible but was now expected to do the opposite and increase troops. In his speech he did in fact order troop increases of 30,000 soldiers.

The next morning's paper in Fort Lauderdale, Florida, carried the story However, the main headline in type font double the size of the Obama name was: *"ROTHSTEIN JAILED. From powerbroker to defendant in $1.2 billion fraud case".* The Rothstein story was also featured nationally.

How did a story about a lawyer "gone bad" outrank in public interest, an important story of national and international interest about which the Nation and the World had been waiting for months? In fact the Rothstein story had been front page news in Fort Lauderdale, where Rothstein operated, almost daily for weeks.

It was indeed an interesting story about a lawyer who had used his charm, connections and guile to run an alleged Ponzi[26] scheme in the amount of over a billion dollars. In the process he had managed to ingratiate himself with the mightiest of the mighty all over the City, County and State and live like an oil sheik, complete with yachts, several mansion and expensive cars.

Tiger Woods' problems

At the same time Mr. Tiger Woods, the most successful single athlete in the world who was elected "Athlete of the Decade" and reputably worth a billion dollars, drove his car into a fire hydrant and a neighbor's car in the very early morning hours. Nobody got hurt. Mr. Woods merely damaged his own car and the neighbor's.

Yet the media followed the story on an hourly basis. Questions were being asked about how and why he did that and about whether or not there was some serious moral flaw that could explain it. Later it became clear that Mr. Woods had been guilty of a number of sexual transgressions with various women. But that was not known at the time.

[26] A Ponzi scheme involves falsely promising high returns to investors and then paying them off with new investor's money.

The Fox News coverage

On the Fox Network Bill O'Reilly Factor, a national and very popular talk show, host Bill O'Reilly asked his guest Bernie Goldberg, *"Why the fascination with the Tiger Woods story?"* Goldberg replied that the media gave the readers what they wanted, but he couldn't explain *why* the readers wanted it.

What accounts for the public fascination with the troubles of Mr. Rothstein, the very early morning driving habits of Mr. Woods, or other things of a similar nature? Things like the severe increase or decrease in the weight of celebrities, or tales about their sexual transgressions, or other human failures of famous people

The answer is *Schadenfreude,* a German word meaning: *the glee we take in other's misfortune.* The Beast in all of us wants to feel good about itself or alternately to just feel good.

We live in a very competitive society. Among us are many very successful people, all of whom have attained higher society grades than most of the rest of us and therefore our "society" appears to regard as somehow "better than we are".

When the "mighty fall" our Beast sees that as proof that they are, at least in some particular way, *"not as good as we are".* That makes our Beast feel good. The alleged criminal behavior of Mr. Rothstein, or the potential moral failure of a Tiger Woods constitute a human failure of character, will power, integrity or whatever in some powerful person that we see as a 'plus' to ourselves[27].

[27] Tabloid magazines are another example of the publicizing of celebrity failures in marriages, weight control, careers, bad aging, etc., that provide so many of us with the same Schadenfreude feeling.

The philosopher's view:

The longshoreman philosopher and author Eric Hoffer wrote: *It is remarkable by how much a pinch of malice enhances the penetrating power of an idea or an opinion. Our ears, it seems, are wonderfully attuned to sneers and evil reports about our fellow men.*

But it is not "nice" to show pleasure in the failure of others. So it is rare indeed that anyone admits that they "enjoyed" seeing another person "go down". Moreover, the Logical Me within us does not take any such pleasure and is often ashamed of the Beast's reaction. That conflict is resolved by silence and often outward denial of the inner glee.

The need to prove one's love

Years ago, a story in the Reader's Digest illustrated this point dramatically. A farmer and his wife went to see a doctor because the wife was very sick. The wife privately told the doctor she didn't care whether she lived or died because her husband of thirty years did not love her and had not said he did in decades.

The husband, talking privately, assured the doctor that he did indeed love his wife very much, but that he was not an emotionally expressive person and had a lot of trouble actually saying "I love you" to his wife.

The wife was badly in need of a blood transfusion, for which the husband hastened to volunteer. Unfortunately, their blood types were not compatible. Nevertheless, the doctor told the wife that her husband loved her dearly and that he wanted to be the blood donor. Neither the husband nor his wife had ever been involved in a blood transfusion. So the doctor was able to set up a scenario whereby the wife and husband were placed in adjoining beds separated by a sheet and were then told the transfusion occurred.

In fact, the doctor stored the husband's blood and gave the wife a transfusion of compatible blood. It was that apparent gesture by the husband that fully convinced the wife that her husband really loved her and repaired a relationship that had gone bad, thus giving the wife reason to want to live, despite her health.

The wife went from feeling very badly about herself as unloved, to feeling good about herself when she perceived herself as loved.

The level of sincere repetition is a matter of individual needs and of the importance of the person giving relative to the receiver. For example, the parent of a learning disabled child would do well to continually reinforce the child's potentially low self-esteem with literally daily positive input. It is also a given that married couples would benefit from daily expressions of love for each other.

The need for appreciation

A true story from the Reader's Digest illustrates the need for appreciation so that a person can feel good about herself. It is about a rancher's wife who fed their ranch hands daily.

She worked hard to make them good meals and never once did she hear a single word of praise. One day she went around the table placing fresh cut hay on each ranch hand's plate. When one of the hands asked, *"What the hell is this?"* she answered, *"Well, I've been feeding all of you for over a year and I ain't heard a word yet to suggest I ain't serving hay."*

Ask yourself – *when was the last time I told my spouse how much I appreciate all he or she does for me and our family? How long have I been taking all the good things my spouse does for granted?*

Identifying good things others do

The things that qualify as good things that can be used by one person to make another feel good about herself depend on age, general ability, and cultures.

For example, a normal child's good things will be measured by how well he listens to his parents and teachers, how well he does in school, and how well he gets along with others, and so on. On the other hand, a child with disabilities who is trying hard to do as much as he can should also be praised for his efforts, regardless of the level of accomplishment or the difficulty of the task.

In other words, whenever praising a child or adult for something they've done well, sometimes the effort and the outcome will not coincide due to ability or skill. Most times it's the effort that we should praise, despite the outcome.

When the learning disabled do better than the non-disabled

My daughter, Claudia, is married to a man named Jay. Both are learning disabled. With a little help, they have learned to manage their finances extremely well. They are proud to have learned to live on a budget, and to remember the things that are essential to sound family and personal finances. As a parent of one and father-in-law to the other, I think it is important to keep praising them on this very important life achievement, and I do.

On the advantage of hiring the learning disabled

As the father of a learning disabled child I have had some involvement with a group supporting the learning disabled. What I found quite surprising is that the learning disabled make *better* employees in many respects than the non learning disabled. The reasons are clear. A learning disabled person usually has much more difficulty overcoming the initial obstacle of being hired than the non disabled.

Employers are often reluctant to hire them for fear that they may not do their jobs well. The learning disabled suffer from low self esteem and a low societal grade. As a result and most unfortunately many feel bad about themselves. But for the same reason getting and keeping a job is more important to the learning disabled than to the non disabled. It is what makes them feel much better about themselves.

That is why when they do get a job within their abilities to do, they will often outscore their non disabled peers in reliability, punctuality, politeness, attitude, etc., *Getting and keeping a job is far more critical to their self image and their ability* <u>*to feel good about themselves*</u> *as well as their financial survival in a world much harder for them to cope with, than the non disabled.*

That is why they often make it an absolutely top priority to keep their job. Moreover as long as they are put in a position they can handle they strive to totally satisfy their employer, and they usually succeed.

What is considered good by the person's peer group?

The things considered good by a person's peer group will usually be the same as those considered good by the society in which the person lives. It will be easy to recognize and praise those good things a person does and thereby make the person feel good about herself.

<u>*What those 'outside society' consider their values*</u>

Some people live outside society, usually because they have little or no choice. These people have established their own peer groups for reasons that will be explained later. Those peer groups may consist of street gangs or fanatical fringe groups such as white supremacists, anti-white groups, and religious fanatics, as well as other extreme groups of one kind or another.

These groups have their own set of values, or things they consider good that are often opposed to the values of society. For example, to a gang member, the normal 'good thing' of obeying the law by turning in a fellow member who committed a crime is viewed as 'ratting out' a family member.

In the gang, doing that is the wrong thing. That is why expecting a gang member to do the right thing by society's values and tell on his buddies rarely works. There may be better ways to persuade gang members to do right, which will be explored later.

The power of position to do good and bad

Our relationships are not all equally important to us. Moreover, the importance of some relationships will change over time. For example, when we are children, our most important relationship is with our parents. Later in life, our most important relationship may become that with our significant other, our best friend, or our boss.

What is important is that the amount of influence for good or bad that one person can have over another is proportional to the importance of the first person's life in the life of the other. This is something we should always keep in mind in trying to make our relationships the best that they can be.

The power of position of one spouse over the other cannot be overestimated. Spouses generally hold a very high degree of power over each other's ability to feel good about themselves. This power properly exercised can result in a blissful relationship. Improperly exercised it can lead to friction, dissent, discord, unhappiness, all too often divorce and unfortunately even homicide.

The 'Power of Position' to make me feel good about myself

In my twenties, I was a fairly good tennis player. I remember being at my club playing a game when a leading citizen, Mr. Schouela, came to watch. This man was believed to be one of the wealthiest men in town. He was a community leader, and a major real estate investor. He saw me play and remarked afterward, "I wish I could play tennis as well as you do."

That statement, coming from that man, made me ***feel very good about myself*** and is clearly remembered over half a century later. *Why is that?* On occasion, I heard the same kind of statements from less prominent people, but I don't recall who they were.

The answer is because the statement coming from that man made me think: *This very important and leading citizen admires something I have and he doesn't. In one small way, I am better than he is, and he has acknowledged that himself!*

The point is that I felt so much better about myself because the compliment came from a man in a position of power, than I would have felt if it had come from less powerful men. His statement fed my ego and my self-esteem. I have no doubt that his ability to make me feel good about myself was indicative of his ability to do so to others and an important contributing skill to his financial success.

Rule #8 – The power of position can greatly influence how we make people feel about themselves.

Rule #9 – We make people feel good about themselves by consistent and sincere acknowledgment of their peer value qualities

Chapter Six

The existence of the Beast within us

Our dual personalities

We have looked at the need for feeling good about oneself and ways to make others feel good about themselves. Can we achieve good relationships just by accepting these facts and then doing these tasks? Unfortunately, it's not that simple. Our brains control what we think, say, and do. However, our brains are not single entities, but rather are made up of three parts.

One part, called the reptilian brain, controls breathing, heart, and liver functions and so on, and does not materially affect our self-esteem. The other two parts of our brain are the limbic or the emotional part, and the neo-cortex or the executive logical part. Together, these two parts are the entities that materially control everything we think, say, and do. Unfortunately, these two parts are sometimes in conflict. It is that conflict that makes us think, say, and do things we sometimes live to regret. *That is why we need to think of ourselves not as one person, or one personality, but rather as two persons living in the same body.*

Because the neo-cortex is the logical part of the brain, we will refer to it here as the ***Logical Me.*** Because the limbic brain is the emotional, illogical part of the brain that can act in a very aggressive, confrontational, and self destructive way, we will refer to it as the ***Beast or My Beast***.

We hope the Logical Me controls our lives. Fortunately for most of us, it usually does. At those times, the Beast, although ever present, is asleep or dormant. When we get very angry, destructive, rude, or improperly aggressive, and we do and say things we regret, it is because the Beast is awake and in control.

Understanding the process; The Bibace working concept of the human brain.

To better understand the process, we need to consider what I call *"the Bibace working concept of the human brain."* The concept calls for an acceptance of the fact that the brain consists in part of two separate and sometimes conflicting personalities, one good and the other often not good and even sometimes truly "evil."

The Strange Case of Dr Jekyll and Mr. Hyde.

Robert Louis Stevenson's novel, *The Strange Case of Dr Jekyll and Mr. Hyde,* was a work that portrayed a split personality. Meaning that within the same person there is both a good and an evil personality, *each being quite distinct from the other.* In the novel, Dr. Jekyll was the good doctor, while Mr. Hyde was the evil monster.

Scientists recognize the brains two separate parts. Though separate in one sense, they are still interconnected in countless ways. One part of the brain is the Dr. Jekyll good doctor personality of the Robert Louis Stevenson's novel–we will call that part the Logical Me. Its job is to make logical decisions. The other part of the brain is the limbic or emotional brain. It tends to react to things in an emotional manner; a manner which ignores any considerations of time, place, cost, or consequences on itself or anyone else. It is the emotional *Mr. Hyde* part of the personality capable of doing great evil. We will think of it here as the Beast.

It is a basic tenet of the Bibace Theory that to some extent we all possess the dual Dr. Jekyll/Mr.Hyde personality. All of us have both the Logical Me and the Beast within us. That is why all of us have the *potential,* given the right set of unfortunate circumstances to do horrible things. How else can we explain genocide, torture, serial killings, murder for profit and revenge, the rape of children, and so many other unimaginable horrors we read about daily?

The two part brain and the obstacle to doing good created by the limbic brain

Initially, both parts of the brain want the same thing. They are both motivated to feel good about themselves and/or to avoid feeling bad about themselves. The problem lies in the reaction of the Beast when it doesn't get what it wants. It is by understanding that reaction that one can control one's Beast and thereby increases one's ability to achieve good relationships.

When the Logical Me doesn't get what it wants, it simply accepts that and moves on. The illogical Beast does not always react that way. In certain circumstances, the Beast will react to the failure of feeling good about itself by settling for behaving in a manner that makes it just feel good. Feel good behavior is usually destructive to itself or others and behavior that will tend to make one feel bad about oneself later.

This fact is the very important difference between *feeling good about oneself* and simply *feeling good.* The first is almost always the result of positive behavior, while the second is often the result of negative behavior.

We feel good about ourselves when we behave in a manner of which society approves, and that is therefore good for everybody. But behavior that causes us to just *feel good* is usually *bad source feel good behavior*. That is because it often involves excesses of food, alcohol, illegal drugs, sexual activity, and whatever else that will provide immediate physical or emotional pleasure regardless of consequences. It can trigger abusive behavior that will hurt others like physical and verbal abuse of others and their property, up to and including arson and murder.

When the Beast is sufficiently frustrated with a lack of feeling good about itself, it 'settles for feeling good'. It does so by taking over the individual's thoughts and actions in a manner opposed to logical goals and the best interests of the individual. Moreover, it can do so in such a secret and invisible manner as to go completely unnoticed by the Logical Me.

Flip Wilson and Geraldine's "The Devil made me do it"

This is an example of what happens when individuals who have done bad things and then say, "*I just can't understand how I could ever have done such a thing!*" This was the repeated claim of innocence made by Flip Wilson's seventies sitcom Geraldine character, in explanation of her repetitious immoral behavior. She would say: "*It's not my fault! The Devil made me do it!*"

Geraldine was talking about the "Devil" within her as if he were an outside force, similar to a man with a gun, forcing her to misbehave. Yet there is no question that in some cases, at least, Geraldine would be as unable to exercise her own free will as if she were facing a man with a gun.

My own "Devil" almost made me do it

I still remember vividly an incident that happened to me over 60 years ago, when I was only 13 years old. I had been fighting with another older boy, and had received the worst of the fight. I recall shortly afterwards standing in front of a newsstand waiting for a streetcar and still in a white rage from the event. The newsstand's newspapers were weighed down by a heavy metal tire jack. There was some question as to whether the boy I had been fighting would seek to continue the fight. I still distinctly remember (with considerable distress) my very definite intention of picking up the jack and smashing the boy's skull if he came after me again.

To this day, I believe I would have killed him. Yet this was not a stranger. It was a friend I knew well and had played tennis and chess with and socialized with regularly at a club to which we both belonged. I have never felt that way before or since. Nevertheless, even feeling that way for a single second remains a very distressing experience.

It did provide me with the insight to understand that if I, a person who has never had any trouble of any kind with the law, before or since that incident, *could, under the right set of circumstances,* be prepared to kill a friend over a boyhood fight, what does that say about others in even more provocative circumstances?

Let us call the *Ronald Bibace Theory of Personality,* Stage One of the new approach to solving relationships problems, after which, we move to the following Stages: Stage Two: Establishing that it is the Beast that reacts to a particular situation and is in control of the Logical Me. Stage Three: Explaining how to make a particular individual feel good about him or herself.

Stage Four: Explaining how to use the "magic switch" or speedy solution, whenever applicable.

Rule #10 – Think of yourself and others as having two personalities-one logical,(the Logical Me) and the other not (The Beast)

Rule #11 – Always remember the power of the Beast to take over the Logical Me in you and others

Chapter Seven

The Power and Nature of the Beast

The 'Beast' at its worst is brutal, harsh, unsympathetic, and unforgiving. It is neither smart nor logical. It has no sense of right and wrong, nor any sense of time. The Beast is only aware of the here and now. It acts and reacts harshly and spontaneously to get what it wants. It is generally incapable of considering consequences to itself or to others, including loved ones. It seeks to satisfy its goals at all times. Like an unruly child, it wants what it wants when it wants it!

The Beast operates at the conscious and subconscious mind level[28] and can pick up cues of which the Logical Me remains unaware. It is like a dog or a bat that can hear sounds at pitch levels inaudible to the human ear. It can also sense everything that the Logical Me[29] can sense. The Beast sometimes operates like a heroin addict in need of a fix, although that which satisfies its addiction may not always be

[28] Lifeboost reports on hubpages.com, that while the conscious mind can process 40 bits of information per second, the subconscious mind can process 40 million in the same time.

[29] This tends to explain what is sometimes referred to as "gut reaction," referring to a feeling of discomfort about a situation or a business deal that is unsupported by any apparent information. It seems the subconscious brain has picked up on some "below the radar" cue, which caused it to provide a level of discomfort as a signal to the "gut." That kind of cue appears to be very reliable.

harmful. The intensity of the addiction will vary with the level of present and stored emotional satisfaction, or what is referred to here as emotional currency, which it has received.[30]

The Beast's addiction, however, is not to heroin or cocaine, or any other controlled addictive substance. Its addiction is to ***the need to feel good about itself!*** If it cannot satisfy that need, it will settle for just ***feeling good.*** Both the Beast and the Logical Me want to satisfy the same need, but only the Beast will, under certain circumstances, substitute the ***need to feel good*** for the missing need to feel good about itself. It is in an attempt to satisfy that need through 'bad sources' that the Beast may, and sometimes will, do itself and others great harm.

The Power of the Beast

The Beast within us can have enormous power. In the "right" circumstances it is capable of making us do some or all of the following things that are very much against our own best interests and the best interests of those near and dear to us as well as society as a whole:

- *It can cause us to kill in a rage*
- *It can cause us to be physically violent to others without logical cause.*
- *It can cause us to bully and intimidate others*
- *It can cause us to be verbally abusive to others and even to those near and dear to us*
- *It can cause us to pursue disastrous life and financial decisions*
- *It can cause us to be in denial of disagreeable truths*

[30] That satisfaction is termed "emotional currency" by this writer and will be the subject of later chapters.

- *It can cause us to turn to one or more of greed, gluttony, lust, envy, anger, laziness and excessive pride, (The seven cardinal sins)*
- *It can cause us to destroy the very relationships on which we depend for our happiness and success in life*
- *It can cause us to hate*
- *It can prevent us from forgiving*
- *It can cause us to blame everybody but ourselves*
- *It can permanently prevent us from recognizing and correcting our mistakes.*
- *It can prevent us from using our own intelligence or listening to that of others.*

Visualization of the Limbic Brain as the metaphorical Beast

Visualization is an excellent aide to understanding complex issues. In the context of the Bibace Theory, we think of the limbic brain as the Beast. It is an all-powerful, irrational, wild, and beastly clawed creature inside the skull; its claws sunk deeply into the Logical Me, invisible to all, including the individual self as well as outsiders.

However, the Logical Me feels no pain and is almost always unaware that it may be under the Beast's control. The Beast can be pictured in a cage to which there are only two levers. One lever is labeled "Feel Good About Myself." The other is labeled "Feel Good." The Feel Good lever may trigger a few activities such as exercising or playing sports that are good. That is what I call the good source feeling good.

Pressing the Feel Good lever, however, is far more likely to result in bad behavior such as excessive eating or drinking, substance abuse, sexual excesses, violence, whether verbal or physical to others or even to oneself. That is the 'bad source feeling good'.

Most of the time, and for most people, the Logical Me succeeds in providing a sufficient level of feeling good about itself to satisfy the Beast. Alternatively, even if the desired feeling is insufficient, the Beast may not be sufficiently aroused to react negatively.

From time to time, and with some people, the Beast will be aroused to action and press the *feel good* lever. When that happens, the Logical Me obeys the invisible command by thinking, saying, and doing all things necessary to achieve the goal of feeling good. It often does so without being aware that it was obeying the Beast's command. At best, the Logical Me will occasionally sense its lack of control by remarking after the fact, "*I can't understand why I did that!*"

The Holocaust museum and the "faceless Germans"

I visited the Holocaust Museum in Israel some years ago. The Museum contains a large mural sculpture showing German soldiers marching Jews off to death camps. One extraordinary feature of the exhibit is that the artist left the German soldiers faceless. The Museum guide explained that the artist considered the Holocaust such a completely inhuman and barbaric act, that in his mind, the perpetrators were not "human" at all. Leaving the soldiers without faces was intended to show that.

Unfortunately, the idea, though clearly deeply felt and well intended, conveys the wrong message. The correct message is that the German soldiers were human.

The truth is that even otherwise normal human beings can be so far under the control of the Beast within them that they can do things that ordinarily they would regard as completely beyond the pale.

The Rwandan genocide

As recently as 1994, nearly half a century after the Holocaust, the Rwandan Genocide occurred. On that occasion, between 500,000 and 1,000,000 members of Rwanda's Tutsi tribe were killed by the rival Hutu tribe. The whole thing happened over no more than about 100 days. That means that between 5,000 and 10,000 people were being killed every single day![31]

Can anyone still question that there is a Beast within all of us that is capable of horrible, unthinkable atrocities under the right circumstances? Were the German people during World War II and the Rwandans during 1994 so far removed from the humanity of the rest of us that we cannot conceive of anyone else doing such things? What about the "ethnic cleansing" and the rapes and murders that occurred in the recent Yugoslav civil war? Are the perpetrators of those atrocities also somehow subhuman? The evidence strongly suggests otherwise.

Hitler's rise to power

Hitler's rise to power is another example of the universal need to feel good about ourselves. In 1918, Germany had just lost World War I and been forced to sign harsh surrender terms. What followed was a period of chaos and wild inflation, unemployment, and general unrest. There was a general malaise in the nation and the Germans felt very bad about themselves.

Hitler's message was, "*Raise your heads. We are a great people who have been betrayed by the traitors and the Jews among us. When we get rid of these people, all will be well.*"

[31] There are continuing reports from the Congo that similar atrocities are currently going on even at the time of this writing.

The Germans were only too happy to hear that message. *It made them feel good about themselves.* The war they lost was not their fault – it could be blamed on others.

Hitler found a scapegoat in the Jews and the alleged traitors among the Germans. The Germans supported Hitler enthusiastically. Doing so made them feel better and better about themselves. As a result, on September 1, 1939, their Fuehrer launched World War II by attacking Poland. A war that resulted in the death of some 60 million people, including the murder in gas chambers of some 11 million people of whom 6 million were Jews.

Hitler's popularity with the Germans when they were winning.

It is also interesting that as long as the Germans were winning the war, from the invasion of Poland in 1939 to the disaster for Germany at the battle of Stalingrad in February 1943, the Germans were feeling better and better about themselves. They regarded themselves as invincible. They had demonstrated to the world that indeed for a long time they were. Serious plots to remove Hitler did not surface until 1944. So, for as long as the Germans felt good about themselves because they were winning, no decent German desiring to remove Hitler had the slightest hope of success.

Is it too much to expect that all this would not have happened if greater care had been paid to avoid making an entire people feel as bad about themselves as the Germans did after World War I? I think not. However, even if the fault does not lie entirely with the German people for what happened, they must still take responsibility for what they did. Fortunately, they have done that. So must each and every one of us when our Beast takes over our lives.

Hitler's desire to destroy Germany and the Germans

A further insight into the importance of feeling good about oneself is the reported reaction of Hitler in the last days of the war. To make himself feel good about himself, Hitler was single-minded in the belief that he was Germany's savior; that if they conquered the world, it was thanks to him.

But what if the war was lost? Hitler's attitude when he realized that the war was lost was not to blame himself. On the contrary, he believed that he had been betrayed by traitors and the German people. Moreover, he decided that under those circumstances the German people did not deserve to survive at all.

To that end, he instructed his armament's minister and good friend Albert Speer, to destroy all the infrastructures in Germany. Hitler wanted bridges, railroad stations, power plants, dams, etc. destroyed so that the "unworthy German people" would all die.

Speer saves the Germans

Albert Speer disobeyed the order and actually tried to kill Hitler in the last days of the war. He was also the only very high ranking German who took full responsibility for his participation in the crimes against humanity that the Germans perpetrated on the world. For his crimes Speer served twenty years in prison.

What is important is to recognize Hitler's need to feel good about himself no matter what happened. That was a need that caused him to fervently believe himself as the either the Savior of his Fatherland, or as the Avenging Angel destroying his worthless and betraying people. In both cases, he remained a great man in his own subjective reality.

The Milgram experiment; torture under official approval

In 1961, pretending to do a lab experiment, Yale Psychologist Stanley Milgram hired people off the street to press a button they were led to believe would electrically shock another participant hired for the experiment and told to pretend the shock was real. The astounding results show that the average person would keep torturing a perfect stranger, even to death, as long as they believed they were acting in accordance to their society's values.

There was an aura of respectability, and of doing the right thing by society's values, created by a major university involved in what appeared to be a valid experiment. That is what provided the torturers with a sufficient level of feeling good about themselves to overcome their natural revulsion to torture.

It is extremely unlikely that the torturers would have proceeded as they did if all they had been offered was more and more money for higher levels of torture. Payment for the torture versus a valid experiment would have been seen as not acceptable.

That experiment is dramatic proof of the lengths to which average people will go if they are acting in a manner they believe is okay with the values of the society in which they live. It also explains why people who grow up in particular societies can grow up hating entire groups of people for their ethnicity, religion, or the color of their skin, even when they have never met a single member of these hated groups in their lives. They do it because it is part of the belief system of the society in which they live. They feel good about themselves when their beliefs are the same as those of their peers.

The Power of the Beast to destroy capital

Losing money makes usually makes us *feel bad about ourselves*. The more responsible we feel for the decision that caused the loss, the worse we feel. That is because there are two aspects to losing money that affect us emotionally. The first is the direct result of having less money than before. That feeling remains the same in all situations. The second is the impact on our Beast (or our ego) of having been responsible for the loss. That will change depending on how responsible we see our decisions as having been the cause of the loss.

Fear of loss greater motivator than prospect of gain

When it comes to finances, fear of loss is a greater motivator than prospect of gain[32]. That often means that the *fear of feeling bad about oneself* will often motivate behavior that is completely illogical, just to delay that feeling for a while.

The Beast destroys the last $600,000

In Montreal in 1962 I was involved in a real estate brokerage operation in which my firm was selling homes in several projects for a major local Corporation. Times got bad and the Corporation was losing about $100,000 a week. The owner of the Corporation still had other assets that were not at risk. Nevertheless he took his last $600,000 and invested it in the company. That investment bought him another 6 weeks before he had to declare bankruptcy anyway. Nor was there any logical reason at the time to suppose that the $600,000 would do more than delay the prospects of bankruptcy.

[32] *The Economist Jan 16, 2010- Designing rewards – Carrots dressed as sticks*

So why would anybody dump his last $600,000 (equivalent to at least $3 to $4 million in 2010 dollars) in a logically hopeless attempt to save his company? The only explanations is that the owner *felt so bad about himself* at the thought of going bankrupt that he was willing to invest his last penny to delay that feeling. His Beast would not let him make the rational decision.

The Beast triples losses.

In another situation a friend asked my advice on a real estate investment he had made. He had invested $80,000.00 to buy an apartment for $780,000 which was then under construction. By the time the apartment was ready for closing the market had gone bad and the apartment was worth much less than he had paid. He had two choices. Close on the apartment and be at risk for more money, or walk away from the deal and accept the loss of $80,000.00. I told him that he needed to ask himself a simple question: *Was the apartment worth at least the $700,000.00 he would now have to commit? If not, he should walk away. The original $80,000.00 was already gone forever. Thinking any other way was like the gambler who keeps losing more and more money at the table because he thinks "the table owes him".*

He knew that the apartment was clearly not worth anywhere near even the $700,000.00. Plain logic (and his *Logical Me*) would therefore dictate that he walk away. But logic is not what the Beast believes in. The friend closed on the deal. A year later he disposed of the property after taking an additional loss equal to about 3 times what the original loss would have been.

What happened? Again the fear of loss which is also *the fear of feeling bad about oneself* was so great, that the friend was willing to pay a further very substantial price to delay feeling bad about himself. His Beast got him!

The power of the Beast in one person to cause others to lose money needlessy.

We have seen how our own Beast can make us lose money. But what about the power of someone else's Beast to do the same thing? Does that power exist? Unfortunately it certainly does. This is a true story about just such a situation told to me by a friend recently. He had just finished reading an earlier edition of this book when he recognized what had happened decades earlier as just such a loss. Here is his story.

In the 1970s, following the successful release in theatres of a documentary titled *In Search of Noah's Ark,* a Limited Partnership raised several hundred thousand dollars to finance a similar production, based on finding the lost land of Atlantis. There was one very large investor, known in such business ventures as the 'angel,' and a dozen smaller ones who participated in the deal. Initially, the deal looked great. Two years of solid research produced a script which the major film studio Warner Brothers liked enough to offer the company a pre-buy. Then, at the very last minute, Warner backed out and the production, out of cash, seemed sunk.

Out of nowhere, a young and very brash new investor walked in and offered enough fresh cash to put the deal back on track, and get the finished film into distribution. There was one catch – the aggressive young dealmaker wanted the senior 'angel' to give up some of his "profit points" on the restructured deal. It is important to understand that no new funds were needed from any of the prior investors *including the 'angel'*, and that the deal would have been an instant total loss to everybody if the offer were rejected.

To the shock and horror of the other original investors, the senior 'angel' rejected the new offer. The production quickly folded at a full 100% loss. What happened? To the senior angel, a millionaire many times over, the potential loss of self-approval, *or the sense of feeling bad about himself,* reflected in ceding points to the brash young newcomer was a much greater hardship than merely losing all the money he had already invested. If the others in the deal had understood that at the time, *which they unfortunately did not,* they might have handled the negotiation very differently (using the principles in this book, for example) and the film might have been made.

The power of the beast to reach illogical conclusions

Choosing a lower salary

If you were asked, "*Would you rather be paid $100,000 or $200,000 for doing exactly the same job?*" the answer would be so obvious that the question would appear either ludicrous or rhetorical. But what if you were asked, "*Would your rather earn $100,000 when all your peers are earning $50,000 for the same job, or earn $200,000 when all your peers are earning $400,000, also for the same job?*" the answer might not be as clear.

The conflict, if you chose the higher amount of $200,000, would lie between feeling good about yourself for being able to earn the $200,000 because of the increased material wealth, and feeling bad about yourself because your peers were earning twice as much as you did. Choosing the lower amount of $100,000 would give you less material wealth *but make you feel a lot better about yourself as the highest paid among your peers.*

A survey was taken some years ago on this matter and surprisingly, or perhaps not, a majority elected to make less than they could otherwise, *as long as they made much more than their peers!* In other words, the Beast is happier making *half the salary* but twice as much money as the peers, because the Beast *"feels better about itself"* than if it were making *twice the salary* but half as much money as the peers.

That is also one reason why so many companies insist on keeping salaries and bonuses as confidential as they can. A person may be delighted with a 25% annual bonus. But may quickly become disenchanted and even belligerently quit, if she discovers that a "peer" doing similar work was rewarded with a 50% bonus!

The Power of the Beast to cause the abandonment of money owed

A friend of mine I will call Karl, now deceased, was a master in his youth of both chutzpah and the art of avoiding payment of debt. He had learned how to make his creditor's Beast make the creditor *feel so bad about himself* that the debt was eventually forgotten.

Karl was a tall good looking charismatic man. But if one asked if he were honest, the best response might be: *He isn't a fanatic about it!* Or to put it another way, Karl was acquainted with a lot of people. Some trusted him, some knew him. But those who knew him didn't trust him and those who trusted him didn't know him.

Karl had a habit of borrowing small sums of money from his friends which he promised to repay within a week or two, but generally did not. Karl's basic technique to avoid repaying his debts were as follows: When asked for repayment he would pretend to be angry and say: *What are you in such a rush for? Do you see me leaving town that you feel the need to harass me for the money?*

This made the creditor really *feeling bad about himself* for having apparently "insulted" Karl. It would make the creditor stop asking and wait for Karl to offer to repay. That offer rarely came. Eventually, sometimes when the debt was as much as two years past due, the creditor would tentatively say: *Karl, do you remember the $50 I lent you two years ago that you never repaid?* To which Karl would jokingly reply: *Aren't you ashamed to bring up a matter that is that old and should be forgotten. It's ancient history. Let's just forget about it.* The debt remained unpaid.

The final chutzpah – the blackbird returning the corn

There is a joke about two Indiana corn farmers discussing the latest scarecrows each had erected to protect their crops from blackbirds. The first said: *I have not lost a single ear of corn since I erected my scarecrow.* The second said: *You think that's good? Since I erected mine the blackbirds are returning the corn they stole last year.*

There came a time when Karl borrowed $100 from one of his good friends, promising to pay it back on the first of the next month. On the day in question he cut a check to his friend. The check bounced. Karl apologized and issued a new check for the first of the next month. That check bounced too. This went on for several months.

Finally the friend decided on a plan. He knew Karl made his car payment for $200 on the fifteenth of the month. So he held back depositing his check until the 15th and this time the bank paid it. *But that was not the end of it.*

Karl's car payment check bounced because his friend's check had depleted the account. He called his friend furious and said: *For several months now I have been giving you a* *check on the first of the month that bounces, which I then replace with a new check. You and I both know that the new check will probably also bounce and that is how the matter has been handled. Now you have the gall to make your deposit in a very sneaky way, just before you know I have to make my car payment. My car payment bounced. The company will repossess my car and I will not be able to make a living and it will all be your fault. Give me back that $100 right away!*

He succeeded in making his friend *feel so bad about himself* that the friend returned the $100! Talk about chutzpah, and talk about the power of the Beast to force illogical decisions on a person.

The Power of the beast to cause us to hate and never forgive

When we are hurt by others we are made to *feel bad about ourselves.* That happens because we feel cheated, abused, 'done wrong', and made to feel weak and powerless because we feel we were treated unfairly. Our weakness, helplessness, or inability to respond or obtain justice makes our Beast as well as our Logical Me feel *bad about ourselves.*

A battle often occurs between our two "selves". The Logical Me often tries to "be kind and reasonable". It thinks such kind and reasonable thoughts as: *Nobody's perfect. Or, to err is human, to forgive divine.* Or even perhaps: *The hurt was unintended.* Or most rationally*: Hating another just hurts the hater, adversely affecting her peace of mind and even perhaps harming her health with ulcerous thoughts.* The Logical Me thinks: *My best bet is to either forgive and forget, or at least think: It is what it is. I need to accept it and move on with my life.*

Not so the Beast. The Beast wants revenge. If it cannot achieve it in reality it seeks a feeling of satisfaction and feels better about itself by reliving the injustice and repeatedly condemning the perpetrator, perhaps even punishing the perpetrator in a mental fantasy. It does so both internally and externally. It does so internally by thinking often on the injustice and the culpability of the offender. It does so externally, by repeatedly recounting the offense to anyone who will listen.

The Beast cannot forgive. To the Beast, forgiving is *rewarding the offender instead of punishing him!* That often remains true even when the offender has made restitution for the harm and apologized. In our culture criminals who have paid their debt to society can be reintegrated in the community. In our minds that does not always follow for those who offend us.

My own inability to forgive

You will have seen from my own life history that my own Beast would never let me forgive my own parents for my perception that they had 'condemned me to death' at the age of seven. My 'Logical Me' would argue that I misread what happened; they never intended to do that; they were desperate to control my hyperactive behavior; nobody understood that I suffered from a medical problem not intentional bad behavior; my mother had apologized profusely; and both my parents had shown their love in many other ways.

My Beast would respond: *None of that matters.* The damage, the hurt and the harm they did to me was severe, lifelong and completely inexcusable. There was no forgiveness possible! That response of squarely placing the blame on my parents 'forever' made my Beast *feel good.*

The wife's inability to forgive her husband's financial errors.

This is a true story about a couple I will name John and Mary. John was a fairly successful business man who had made a number of bad financial decisions later in life. Unfortunately, those decisions resulted in the couple having to reduce their standard of living and face harsh economic circumstances. Mary had to go out and work and take over the family finances. She managed the family's reduced circumstances well, but never forgave nor forgot what she deemed her husband's "inexcusable errors".

Her Beast was forever repeating to all who would listen how badly John had mismanaged their financial affairs and how relatively well she had done after that. As a result both John and Mary became bitter and continued to live unhappily together only because financially they had no other choice.

The answer to the old joke

There is an old joke that is phrased as a question and goes like this: *Why do we spend money we don't have, to buy things we don't want, to impress people we don't like?*

The answer is that our Beast makes us do those things in order to feel good. It is a key and powerful *bad source* feel good cause.

One way to overcome the illogical Beast

How I helped a Cambridge PhD feel good about himself.

One of the friends I made in my first year at UBC was a man called Chris who was had earned a PhD at Cambridge University, England. We met in the first week of school and he told me about an experience he had as soon as he arrived in Vancouver.

The all knowing taxi driver

He had taken a taxi from the airport to the University and had an interesting conversation with the taxi driver. He had found that the taxi driver spoke with great authority on all subjects and seemed to be very sure he knew a great deal about everything. Chris on the other hand, although a man who had earned a PhD in Chemistry at one of the most prestigious universities in the world, felt he knew very little about the world. The conversation with the taxi driver emphasized that situation and made him *feel bad about himself.* Yet the taxi driver was a high school dropout! He wondered aloud how that could be.

I was able to tell him and to overcome his Beast's ability to make him feel relatively ignorant. What we think we know can be thought of as a fraction, the numerator being our actual knowledge, and the denominator being *what we know there is to know.* Thus the more one actually knows the more one gets to realize how much there is to know, and therefore ***relatively speaking*** how little one actually knows.

That means the more we actually know the more we realize how little we know. Another way of saying the same thing is that the "fraction" which represents what we realize we know keeps getting more and more unfavorable. That also means that the less we know the more we feel we know it all!

That explanation satisfied my friend because he understood that his feeling that he knew very little was a clear indication that he knew far more than most people who think they know it all. That made him *feel good about himself.*

The 'Mesmerizing'[33] partner as the Beast's excuse for losing arbitration.

This is a true story about two long term partners who had worked together for 15 years. One of the two was a more skilled advocate and usually right whenever the two disagreed over some issue. Initially the approach for the two (who got along well) was to agree to seek a third mutually acceptable person to do a "friendly" arbitration. Regrettably for the relationship, these 'arbitration' sessions almost invariably favored the more skilled advocate.

The loser in the arbitration *feeling very bad about himself* for consistently being found wrong, satisfied his Beast by declaring that his partner was 'mesmerizing' the arbitrator. He said: *It's not that you are right it's just that you are so skilled an advocate that you can persuade anyone that black is white! You 'mesmerize' them into believing that you are right even though you are wrong!*

His Beast seeking to avoid feeling bad about itself at any cost, persuaded itself that wrong was right, and that right was only made to *look like wrong* by the use of some 'improper' hypnotic power.

Of course the effect of mesmerizing is temporary and should wear off. Even though it in fact never did, because the 'arbitrators' who were also friends, never changed their minds, the losing partner was not persuaded,. He and his Beast had their story and they were 'sticking with it'.

The illogical idea that Logic can be always be relied on as the instrument of change

[33] Mesmerizing definition: hypnotic: attracting and holding interest as if by a spell see wordnetweb.princeton.edu/perl/webwn

The general belief that the Logical Me controls our behavior makes us think that we can change our behavior logically. Unfortunately, that doesn't always happen. The Bibace theory's position is that the Beast exercises far more control over the Logical Me than we realize. It does so, at times, with the Logical Me's knowledge, but not necessarily with its consent. Most often, however, it does so without the Logical Me's knowledge. The part of the Beast's control which we know about is like the visibility of an iceberg above water. In an iceberg, only 10% of the ice is seen above the surface, while the other 90% lies unseen below the surface. The Beast's controlling action is also mostly below the surface of our consciousness.

The major difference between the Bibace Theory and current beliefs is one of degree. Current beliefs seem to attribute most of control of how we behave to the Logical Me's/neo-cortex, not the Beast/limbic brain. This book's view is that in too many cases the reverse is true–*understanding this critical difference is the key to improving relationships.*

The power of the Beast to always blame others

The Beast's desire to feel good about itself at all times and thereby avoid responsibility for its acts is substantial. That is why the Beast successfully seeks to immediately blame somebody or something else the moment that anything bad happens.

Everything that happens to us is the result of a great many earlier things that happened. Therefore whenever a bad thing happens the Beast can immediately blame one of those earlier events.

For example let us assume the Beast has a car accident on the way to the grocery store. It can and will often illogically blame the person on the phone at the house who was responsible for delaying the original plan to leave earlier. Or the 'slow driver' responsible for the Beast having to 'run a red light'. Or the bad weather that impaired visibility. Or whatever else it can think of that 'clears it of responsibility'.

This situation has always existed. As Shakespeare wrote in *Julius Caesar* when Cassius talks to Brutus to argue against the Beast's attitude: *The fault, dear Brutus, lies not in the stars but in ourselves that we are underlings.*

The Romans, like the rest of us, had their own Beast seeking to place blame elsewhere than where it belonged. In those days they blamed 'the stars' or the many 'gods' they believed in. We do the same thing to avoid blame. We just place the blame elsewhere.

Rule #12 – Always be aware of the enormous potential of your Beast to harm you and others and avoid responsibility.

Chapter Eight

Controlling the Beast within ourselves and others. -The Magic Switch

We know that both the Beast and the Logical Me seek to feel good about themselves, and that the Limbic Beast will substitute feeling good when it does not feel good about itself. Therefore, it seems logical that if one could make the Beast feel good about itself in a way that also required it to *change its destructive behavior,* one should be able to stop that behavior. To understand this, we start with a number of givens, which are as follows:

1. *That in a civilized society, being smart is a very good thing. Therefore, recognition in oneself that one is being smart will provide one with the desirable feeling good about oneself.*
2. *That being able to control one's behavior in a smart manner is also a very good thing that will also provide the same effect–feeling good about oneself.*
3. *That both the Beast and the Logical Me know that certain behavior is destructive, but that the Logical Me cares and the Beast does not.*

The magic switch – part one

The idea is to make the Beast become aware of what is occurring. That realization alone should do the trick, because once the Beast becomes aware of the process, and recognizes how smart it must be to do so, it is likely that ***the knowledge, alone,*** like an energy injection, will give the Beast a sufficient shot of good source feeling good about itself to overcome the need for the undesirable activity.

I call this the magic switch because it has the capacity to instantaneously change behavior by 180 degrees. It does this through a mental realization, alone. It can be very quick, virtually effortless, and it seems, can also be long-lasting.

My car driving epiphany

The idea for the magic switch first came to me from a personal experience. For most of my life, I drove safely, but somewhat aggressively. By which I mean I felt the macho thing to do was to *not allow anyone to cut in front of me.* If I saw anyone was about to try, I would close the gap between myself and the car in front of me, to make it impossible for anyone to 'jump the line', and get ahead of me. Not allowing anyone to jump ahead of me *made me feel very good about myself.* I was a macho man! My virility dictated that I not allow anyone try any of that stuff with me!

<u>*Random acts of kindness*</u>

A few years ago, in 2004, I underwent a form of mild epiphany. I determined that it would be very nice for me to begin *performing random acts of kindness.* So now, all of a sudden, I began reversing my previous behavior. I started deliberately slowing down to make room for people who might want to cut in as I approached a highway ramp, or in similar situations.

The extraordinary thing was that the new behavior was providing me the same sense of satisfaction, the *feeling good about myself* that the previous, *exactly opposite* behavior had once provided. My epiphany involved my understanding that that once the new behavior supplied my Beast with the required feeling good about myself satisfaction, there was no longer any conflict, and the change was effortless.

This concept is so important that I am going to repeat it and ask you to reread it again and again: ***Once the new behavior supplied my Beast with the required feeling good about myself satisfaction, there was no longer any conflict, and the change was effortless.*** There are still rare occasions, perhaps three times a year, when I slip back into "macho mode," but only if something significant has disturbed me immediately before the incident. The theory has been anecdotally tested and does seem to work well.

The Jay and Claudia experience

In one dramatic experience, I tested the magic switch technique with my son-in-law and daughter. The happy couple was married in 1992. One evening, some years ago (2005), I asked them both how their marriage was going. Jay said, "Fine." Claudia said, "Fine, *but Jay screams at me a lot.*" I asked Jay why he did that. Jay denied doing it at all. Claudia quietly said: "Yes you do honey. You've been doing it forever." Jay's answer was, "I'm not even aware that I'm doing it, let alone why I'm doing it."

To give you some background information, Claudia and Jay are both minimally learning disabled. He has a good job at the local public library. She works part-time at a major supermarket. Jay grew up in very difficult circumstances because of his disability. He was bullied, robbed, ridiculed, and ostracized in and out of school. He had only one friend all his youth. He never dated until he met Claudia at the age of twenty-three. He met her at a meeting of a group of similarly handicapped young adults created by his mother and one other lady. That group still exists and constitutes the focal point of a very active social circle for the couple.

In 1990, Jay was hit by a car in a hospital parking lot and almost lost his life. He received a substantial settlement. As a result, the couple, who married shortly thereafter, was able to live a comfortable life, buy a house for cash, and with the help of their income from their jobs and the return on the balance of the settlement, they live a very good life.

This is what I said to Jay, "*You grew up with a world of grief. Your limbic brain received very little emotional currency, which is the source of self-esteem. You were beaten, robbed, insulted, and made to feel very badly about yourself. Then you found Claudia. She loves you and thinks you are the best person in the world. You received a substantial cash settlement and married. Now you are a man of substance, with a good job, money in the bank, a wife who loves you, good friends, a social life, and a beautiful home. You have become a big shot.*

Your Beast wants to feel good about itself, and it's not satisfied with all your achievements. So it seeks to feel good as a substitute. I went on to explain: It does so by screaming at Claudia as an exercise of verbal power abuse. That is because a big shot with money, a good job, and a lovely wife can now afford to express himself any way he wants to his wife.

That is how your Beast sees himself as being macho. However, even a person with learning disabilities is smart enough to recognize what is happening when it is explained to him. Even such a man can feel the sense of feeling good about himself that stems from an intelligent awareness of the underlying reasons for the verbal abuse. That realization alone to the effect that you are smart enough to recognize the problem, should suffice to cause you to substantially reduce or even eliminate the need for the screaming."

The entire discussion took less than twenty minutes. Yet, the results were immediate and long-lasting. Jay simply stopped screaming at Claudia. Years later, Claudia reports that the new behavior continues, except for very occasional lapses if Jay happens to be under a lot of pressure or has had a very bad day.

The magic switch – part two

Coping with the Beast in others – the Tourette syndrome

Most of us have learned that it's not *what a person says* that affects us, but rather *how we react to what is said.* For example, the words "*You're bad"* said by a parent to a child, in a serious tone, will make the child feel bad about itself. Whereas, the same words said in jest by a lover will elicit a smile or chuckle.

Therefore, we know it isn't just the words that matter. What about the words and the tone, together? Do we always react in the same way to an aggressive, disagreeable, insulting tone? Not always. For example, there is a mental disorder called Tourette syndrome. People who suffer from it will sometimes make some obscene or very rude remarks.

The targets of these remarks will be very offended and react accordingly, *if they are unaware of the condition.* But those who are aware of the condition, and who realize it is something that the person cannot control, *will not be disturbed by it.* We do not blame others for things they cannot control any more than we would think to blame a baby for soiling itself in public.

The magic switch – part three

This method applies best to people we know. People whom we believe do not really mean what they say when their Beast takes over. The method involves recognizing that the takeover by the Beast of the person's Logical Me is similar to the Tourette syndrome occurrence. The person's Logical Me has temporarily lost control of his logical mind. So the best way to cope with that person is to go with the flow. Or, as some people prefer to call it, "roll with the punches" or "ride with the tide". It can also be thought of as being gracious enough to 'grant another person a shooting license' as my mother did to my father because of his diabetes..

All that means is that one does not use logic in response to an illogical argument when one sees the Beast in control. One lets the storm pass by not responding at all. Alternatively, one can respond by verbally acknowledging and accepting the consequences of the illogical argument and thereby stemming the tide of the Beast's attempt to feel good through aggressive, verbal behavior.

Gilbert's "I'd rather destroy the project" story

Many years ago, I was in France, discussing a major project with a very good friend called Gilbert. Gilbert was a very successful architect/developer. He had never needed or wanted a partner.

At the time, he was faced with major problems in the biggest project he had ever undertaken. Problems that both I, and another very good friend, Tony, were convinced that he would never be able to solve without a partner. Gilbert had asked for our advice. We both pointed out with very clear logic the futility of Gilbert trying to go it alone on this project.

In the midst of the conversation, Gilbert's Beast took over. He loudly and proudly proclaimed, "*I have never needed or wanted partners! Rather than take on a partner, I would rather destroy the whole project!"*

My useless, though totally logical response was, "*Don't be ridiculous! You have invested years and many millions of dollars in this project. You are not about to dump this entire project in the toilet because you refuse to solve your problem by taking on a partner!"*

My good friend, Tony, a wiser man, took another tack. He calmly stated, "*Well, if that what's you want to do, it is one solution!"* Gilbert argued vehemently against my logic. But when Tony[34,35] disarmed his Beast by going with the flow of his totally illogical argument, Gilbert was forced to drop it and return to a logical discussion.

It doesn't always work that way. But it is still the best approach. In this particular case, it didn't help. Gilbert did not take on a partner and the ensuing consequences were not good.

The father's disapproval politely ignored

Many years ago, one of my relatives, while in his early thirties, decided to marry a very charming lady who happened to be a widow with two young children. He knew his father would be unlikely to approve. Still he needed to tell his father about his intentions. He did so. Then he listened with respectful attention to all his father's arguments against the marriage. He did not argue in response. He simply thanked his father for his advice and left. A few weeks later, he announced a wedding date.

His father was literally flabbergasted. He told me, "*I was sure I had convinced him. I don't understand what happened."*

[34] Tony' is Gaston Levy, at the time President of Gillette International and in charge of a large part of Gillette's, (now part of Proctor & Gamble) International business.

[35] He, like me, was born in Egypt and rose through the ranks in a remarkable career which he details in a book he just wrote called: *Beyond the Soul.*

What had happened was similar to the handling of the Beast. The relative simply went with the flow. He knew that no amount of logical argument would persuade his father to approve of his marital choice. He therefore determined to let his father have his say with neither argument nor interruption. After which he did exactly what he both wanted and had a perfect right to do.

All of the evidence and examples support the following conclusion: We can learn to control our Beast and our reaction to the Beast of others by recognizing the ability of everybody's Beast to take over the Logical mind and not allowing that to impact our reactions.

My pride in recognizing that I was wrong

There is one rather extraordinary change in me that internalizing the theories in this book produced. That is the degree of pride I am able to feel in acknowledging that I am wrong. My new philosophy is the following: *Since we all make mistakes, the key to intelligent behavior becomes how quickly we recognize our own mistakes.*

All my life I have tried very hard to be humble. It hasn't worked very well. Like most people, (and even perhaps even more so), *I like to be right all the time.* Also like most people, I (or my Beast) used to feel that admitting to error is admitting to being something of a 'failure'.

However I am now very much aware that it is my Beast that blinds me to the error of my ways. As a countermeasure I now use the 'magic switch' to make myself feel good about myself by recognizing that *I am smart enough* to overcome my Beast's need to refuse to accept error when it is there[36].

That gives my Beast the feel good about itself sense that it craves. That then allows me to look at my own mistakes

[36] I am certainly not saying it works 100% of the time. But there has been a very significant improvement, perhaps as much as 75% of the time.

much more objectively and more easily and therefore far more quickly correct them.

Initial errors corrected swiftly

This is the revised third edition of Relationship Power. The first edition was 'published' but not for sale. It was written as a 'draft' for informal review by a number of people. Even though the reviews were generally favorable, I did receive a certain amount of very justified criticism.

I am happy to report that as a result of my new found 'pride in recognizing when I am wrong' I looked at all the criticisms far more objectively than I would otherwise have done. The evidence of this lies in the fact that I considered virtually all the criticisms constructive and most have been incorporated in this edition.

A rule to live by

If those who read this book get little else out of it, I suggest they attempt to incorporate this one idea into their behavior. *Whenever you are told you are wrong, and don't want to believe it, ask yourself: Is it my Beast or my Logical Me reacting.*

Then remember the following: *Since everybody makes mistakes, my intelligence is shown not by whether I am initially right or wrong but rather by how quickly I recognize and correct my own errors*[37].

Rule #13 – Control of the Beast lies in the 'magic switch' of substituting a positive feeling good about itself resulting from 'superior intelligence' for the negative action the 'feel good' behavior causes.

[37] I would respectfully suggest that those who would dismiss the value of this book confirm the logic of their views with this exercise.

Chapter Nine

Understanding the source of the Beast's Power

You now understand that the Beast operates like a blind, deaf, dumb, and often angry animal interested only in satisfying one of its two needs. The first, which is the same as the Logical Me is to feel good about itself. The second is to simply feel good in order to counteract feeling bad about itself. If the Logical Me is able to behave in ways that make both it and the Beast feel good about themselves, the Beast is quiet and all is well. If not, the Beast may take over the Logical Me and make it act in ways that make it simply feel good, despite the consequences.

Emotional Intelligence or IQ, Emotional Currency, Emotional Capital and 'Interest on Emotional Capital'[38]

The term ***emotional intelligence*** *(sometimes referred to as* ***emotional IQ****)* is a psychological term defined as "*the ability to perceive, express and manage one's own emotions and those of others.*" Or in layman's terms, emotional intelligence defines how well a person handles her emotions and other

[38] Emotional Capital, Emotional Currency and Emotional Interest or Dividends, are used in this context as specifically defined terms. The words may have different meanings in other contexts.

people's. The terms emotional currency, emotional capital and emotional interest or dividends, are defined terms in the context of this book. This is what they mean as used in this book:

Emotional Currency is what I call the love, affection and contribution to self worth and self esteem that one experiences in early life, from birth to adulthood. Although unclear, it seems that the accumulation of *emotional currency into emotional capital* occurs either mainly, or perhaps even *only* in the early years of life, certainly before the age of eighteen. It also seems that the importance is greatest in the earliest years, from birth to five years-old.

'Cash' versus 'coupons'

It seems that emotional currency received in later life is very satisfying when it is received. But it does not seem to have the same level, if any, of ability to be stored. It is as if the emotional currency in early life is like a form of *'self esteem' cash that can be banked.* Whereas emotional currency received in later years is more like *self esteem 'coupons'* that have a short term expiry date

In this respect it seems the brain's ability to create emotional capital through the accumulation of emotional currency is age related. The younger the brain, the easier it is to do. It is almost as if, past a certain age, the emotional *capital* bank account is closed by the brain. After that emotional currency is still very welcome, but *cannot be stored into emotional capital.*

That is because young brains absorb and internalize knowledge like a sponge. For example, everyone knows that the brain learns languages most easily when young. I grew up speaking 4 languages in Egypt. I spoke English, French, Arabic and Italian, as well as a few words of Greek. So did most of my Egyptian born friends of European origin.

We did so with no particular effort and as naturally as if we were learning a single language. None of us ever regarded it as evidence of special skills or intelligence. When I was eighteen, however, and sought to learn Spanish and then Portuguese, the effort was much greater and the result not nearly as good.

Emotional Capital is what I call the *accumulation* of *'emotional currency'.* The concept is similar to the accumulation of monetary income into monetary capital.

Emotional 'Interest on Capital' or 'Dividend on Capital' are the returns of ***'dividends'*** or ***'interest'*** on the ***'emotional capital'*** one has accumulated. That "interest" constitutes an internal source of self esteem and "feeling good about oneself". It can continue to supply the needed sense of feeling good about oneself *internally* even when current *external* emotional conditions do not.

Think of Emotional currency, capital and interest as analogous to money

The analogy or metaphor is to money. A person with ***'emotional intelligence'*** is like a good money manager, who could also be called a man with 'money intelligence'. Such a person can handle his emotions and those of others in the same way that an expert in money management can handle his own funds and the funds of others.

The Beast is controlled by the quantity of stored 'emotional capital'.

The Beast in each of us is controlled by the amount of ***stored emotional capital*** it has received growing up. The bottom line is that the more love and affection received in the early years of one's life the less control the Beast has in later life.

However, if there is little or no accumulation of emotional capital, the Beast tends to be much more aggressive. This is why those unfortunate people who have been brought up in harsh and difficult circumstances have very little *emotional capital*, and therefore no *emotional interest or dividends* to satisfy their Beast when they are faced with difficult times.

The Rule is: *The power of the Beast is inversely proportional to the level of Emotional Capital.*

Therefore the less *emotional capital* the more powerful is the Beast. The more *emotional capital* the less powerful is the Beast and the more powerful the Logical Me.

The heinous crime anecdotal confirmation

I have attempted to verify this theory every time I heard about serial killers, unexplained random shootings, and stories about particularly heinous crimes. To do so, I have checked from published reports as best I can on the level of emotional capital the individual received while growing up. In every single case, I have been satisfied that there has been confirmation of the theory.

There has generally been near zero emotional capital. That offers one excellent explanation as to why the exercise of abusive power, sometimes unto death, satisfies the desire to seek the *bad source feel good* that the Beast craves because it lacks the *emotional capital* to carry it through difficult times.

The "inner source" theory

Some people believe that the feeling of self-worth comes primarily from 'within' oneself. That is sometimes true, but it ignores the question of how and from where the feeling of self-worth originally arose.

No evidence suggests that anyone is born with such feelings. The feelings arise from early nurturing and love. When asked, all the people questioned who felt this way admitted to having grown up in very loving and nurturing environments.

The Beast's bad behavior will range from virtually zero in those people with high self-esteem, to a total takeover in those with low self-esteem. It is similar to the range of security that financial capital can provide That can range from barely keeping one financially solvent, to allowing one to live in the lap of luxury.

My mother's beast

My sister, Margie, enjoyed sucking her thumb as a child. She did it in her sleep and often when she was awake, and even in company, to the utter despair of our mother, Lena. For reasons that have something to do with the possibility of thumb-sucking creating buck teeth and soggy thumbs, my mother was absolutely determined to stop the activity. Despite my mother's attempts, Margie was not persuaded, and did all she could to continue sucking her thumb in secret, when necessary.

My mother was a very gentle lady, beautiful, well-spoken, and refined. I do not recall ever even seeing her really angry, except on this one occasion when Margie had apparently ignored repeated orders to stop sucking her thumb. She kept stopping when Mother was in the room, but immediately began sucking again when our mother left the room. On this occasion, Mother came back unexpectedly and saw Margie, about eight years-old at the time, with her thumb in her mouth.

Our usually gentle mother went totally ballistic Grabbing Margie's thumb in one hand, she reached for a cigarette lighter with the other. She lit the flame and was doing all she could to actually burn Margie's thumb! At the time, I was twelve, and I stood there watching, and like a good son, not interfering with my mother's disciplining of my sister. However, before Mother managed to actually burn Margie's thumb, my aunt, attracted by Margie's screams, entered the room and stopped my mother.

The point of the story is that even as sweet, refined, and very ladylike as my mother was, her Beast could, under the right set of circumstances, cause her to such things as would be deemed criminal in this country–a thing she would undoubtedly have regretted all her life if she had not been stopped.

A quick review

We have seen that good human relationships are dependent on one person making the other person ***feel good about himself.*** To do so, we must sincerely acknowledge those qualities and accomplishments that another does well and are in keeping with the values of their peer group.

We've also learned that a potentially serious obstacle to this goal exists in each and every one of us. That obstacle is the fact that we're not a single, monolithic entity, but rather two separate "entities or personalities" in the same mind and body..

These entities consist of a logical entity, *The Logical Me,* and *the Beast,* in this context, because of its potential highly destructive and equally illogical potential. The Beast can and does take over the Logical Me under certain circumstances.

What are some of the factors that may trigger the Beast to take over the Logical Me?

There are many factors that can trigger a Beast takeover. In extreme cases, it can happen without any apparent trigger. Some people are unfortunate enough to walk around like a gun with a 'hair' trigger, which the slightest provocation may cause to go off.

Here are some examples of triggers:

Major and minor triggers

The same "trigger" may appear major to some people and minor to others, depending on their own Beast's level of control. Here is a list of both kinds:

- *An outright threat, insult or challenge by one person to another; one person threatening another with violence over a parking space; one person challenging another to a fight in a bar over some disagreement; one person calling another some derogatory word relating to ethnicity, sexuality, or physical appearance and so on. Unwanted physical contact, such as a blow or inappropriate touching;*
- *A push in anger against a person who inadvertently stumbled onto another; an inappropriate sexual touching of a person.*
- *A very harsh reprimand by a person in some degree of control of another; a severe dressing down by a boss of his employee, particularly in the presence of others; the same by a parent to a child, or one spouse to another.*
- *Failure to respond appropriately to some word or action by another.*
- *Failure to respond lovingly to loving words by one's spouse or significant other.*

- *Failure to react favorably and enthusiastically to another's obvious major effort to please.*
- *Any attitude by one person deemed objectionable by another.*
- *The continuing or even occasional presence of a one person's disapproving or generally negative attitude toward another.*
- *Failure by an employer to provide an expected or promised benefit to an employee.*
- *Failure by one spouse or forgetting a promise to do something for the other spouse, or an important date in the relationship, like an anniversary.*
- *The absence of some positive expected reaction to another.*
- *Failure by one person to greet another with expected enthusiasm.*
- *Failure to show expected levels of gratitude and appreciation by one person for another's efforts in pleasing the first.*

The effect of the trigger

What effect will the trigger factors have on a particular person? The answer is dependent on the particular Beast's level of self-esteem or emotional capital. Let's examine a few examples:

<u>*Mahatma Gandhi*</u>

If there is a high degree of emotional capital or self esteem, a person might be able to take a lot of negative activity directed at him such as verbal abuse, perhaps even some physical abuse, without reacting in kind. This is because his own internal approval system is enough for him to continue feeling good about himself without the need to show any further external word or action.

Mahatma Gandhi, the great proponent of non-violence, was the perfect example of such a man. Of course, there are very few Mahatmas in this world. At some point in time, even a Beast with a great deal of emotional capital may very well react badly.

In 1945, after World War II, Gandhi wanted to free India from British colonial rule. Gandhi understood human nature very well. He said, "I am ready to die but not kill anyone for my beliefs. So we will resist the British occupation and suffer the pain of reprisals from the British. It will hurt, but it is through our pain that the British will see that they are wrong and must leave."

Gandhi knew and relied on the fact that people who oppress others who do not even resist the oppression cannot but help feel badly about themselves. It was in part on the need to relieve that feeling that Gandhi expected the British to "just leave India." They did.

If we possess a low level of self-esteem or emotional capital, we may have our Beast often looking for an excuse for an argument or a fight. The Beast regards it as important to assert its own superiority wherever it goes.

Because of low self-esteem, the Beast attempts to compensate by exercising abusive power of one kind or another. It is so anxious to assert its superiority that it will often verbally attack people it just met. It subconsciously fears they will attack it if it doesn't attack first.

The person with this kind of low self esteem or emotional capital has received very little, if any, "emotional currency" growing up. He may also have had large doses of the exact opposite. He may have been beaten regularly, abused verbally and sexually, made to feel completely inadequate, and so on.

Moreover, and most unfortunately, the Beast's anti-social reactions trigger more and more bad reactions from others, which in turn make all relationships even worse. This creates a very sad and sometimes deadly cycle. A cycle that sometimes ends in the wholesale killing of complete strangers, and then one's self in a last desperate and hopeless attempt to escape the feeling bad about oneself.

My own Beast's activities – Mr. Putdown

I grew up suffering from ADHD. Except for a few exceptions that included a number of close friends I was very fortunate to have, but did not include my parents, I felt totally unloved. I had very little emotional capital to keep my Beast at bay. I was very much under my Beast's control. I was however, reasonably bright, somewhat charismatic, possessed a quick mind, and an excellent command of the English language. I was also lucky enough to enjoy a high society grade. Using such tools as nature had given me, my Beast was forever on the lookout to try *and feel good about itself by putting other people down*. I became Mr. Putdown. I did this in many ways. One way was by finding derogatory nicknames for my friends.

Scarecrow

One particular name I gave a school companion and lifelong friend was "Scarecrow." His given name was Henry, and he did not appreciate the nickname I chose for him. He was tall, slim, and had a thin face and long arms. The nickname fit him perfectly. So much so that he was never able to rid himself of it. It did not matter that he kept saying, "My name is Henry.

Don't call me Scarecrow." He passed away recently, some 60 years after he had been nicknamed Scarecrow, and some people said, "Isn't it sad? The Scarecrow died."

There were others I christened with unflattering nicknames, some of which are not fit to print here. Many stuck for years. Of course, I was not immune from the same treatment. I happen to have a somewhat larger posterior than I would have chosen for myself. That earned me the nickname from some people of "Big ass."

My outrageous behavior in Arabic class

As a student at Victoria College in Alexandria, Egypt, I attended regular classes in Arabic. The teacher, a man named Mr. Louca was a nice fellow who looked indulgently upon my somewhat outrageous behavior in his class. I would speak out freely anytime I wanted, without bothering with the formality of raising my hand for permission. I would also make remarks unrelated to the matters at hand. Because he liked me, he would indulge me.

But now and again I would push the envelope too far and he would say, "That's it, Bibace! I'm putting you down for one hour detention." He would then take up his pencil and write my name down on his detention list. That is when I did the unthinkable and got away with it. I would go quickly from my desk to his and while removing my name by crossing it off the detention list, I would say, "What are we talking about? Who wants to talk detention? Let's quickly remove my name (as I did it). Let's put the detention sheet back in the drawer (as I did that). Let's get on with the class and forget all this detention nonsense."

Mr. Louca would smile at my outrageous behavior, but let me get away with it. I very much enjoyed my "position of power" as the only student who got away with this behavior. It made me feel very good about myself.

Then one day a good friend of mine, Raymond, tried the same thing and looked like he was getting away with it. I sensed danger. I felt that if anyone else tried the same gambit successfully that would end it for everybody, particularly me. I stood up in apparent outrage and said, "What the hell is Raymond doing? He has no business arguing with you when he gets detention."

Mr. Louca looked at Raymond and said, "He's right (meaning me). You will get your detention for one hour." To which poor Raymond protested, "But when Bibace does it you let him get away with it."

I jumped up, furious at this new threat to my position and stated, "Raymond is arguing again with you, Mr Louca. For that new offense he deserves *an extra hour* of detention!" Mr. Louca replied: "Bibace is right. Raymond you now have two hours of detention!"

After which Raymond fell silent for good, and my position was never again threatened by anyone. The point is that somehow because Mr. Louca liked me and found my antics entertaining, he felt good about himself indulging me, and the resulting attitude made me feel very good about myself.

Rule #14 – The Beast is controlled by the level of emotional capital received in early life.

Chapter Ten

The Internalization

Internalization is the process whereby behavior becomes a part of the automatic and subconscious reaction to situations as opposed to consciously thinking about how one is behaving. The Free Online Dictionary definition[39] is *"To take in and make an integral part of one's attitudes or beliefs."* The key to internalization is repeating behavior *consciously* until it becomes *subconscious.*

The point is that only after internalization can one reach the highest automatic level of correctly reacting to one's own Beast as well as that of others, and thereby optimize one's relationships.

Examples of internalization in life include learning how to walk, learning how to drive, learning how to play sports, and learning how to play cards. The more steps involved and the greater the relationships between the steps, the harder it is to internalize the method.

Public speakers are taught: First, tell them what you are *going to tell them.* Second, tell them what *you are there to tell them.* Third tell them what *you just told them.* The point being that only by repeatedly making your point to your audience in

[39] Free Online Dictionary definition downloaded on 12/8/09 from www.thefreedictionary.com

a speech can you hope to have them remember and hopefully internalize it.

Let's look at some examples:

Walking: Normal babies learn to walk between the ages of around ten months and two years. They do so instinctively, in part, but also because they experience what it feels like to try to stand and walk, fall, try to stand again, and so on. Eventually, they begin to walk hesitantly, but without falling much. Then they learn to walk confidently without falling at all.

Driving: Initially, driving can be a frightening experience. For the first time, one is in charge of a two-ton vehicle capable of moving very quickly that has been known to kill people and to have people in it be killed. One learns the preliminaries–Sit in the seat, put on your seat belt, put the key in the ignition, start the car, release the brake, put the car in gear, look carefully at where your are going, slowly drive into the street, drive within the speed limits, stay in your lane, signal before turning, and so on. Initially, some speak to others in the car as little as possible, lest that disturb their concentration. At first, one needs to go over the rules carefully in one's head every time one gets behind the wheel. But after a while, confidence grows, *internalization occurs*, and one can drive virtually "automatically". That is because the subconscious mind has taken over the "routine" aspect of driving. The conscious mind has stopped handling that aspect of driving and is geared to respond primarily to emergencies.

Bridge: The game of bridge is an excellent example of the essence of internalization as well as its difficulties. Bridge is a game played by four people. Every player receives thirteen cards. A bidding process occurs in which each player bids according to the strength of his hand and his perception of the strength of everybody else's hand to make a contract. After which the hand is played. In order to know how to bid and what to bid, it is initially necessary to count points assigned to the cards. Subsequently, it is necessary to listen carefully to each of the other players' bid. That means that in the bidding process alone there is a requirement to make an adjusted assessment *after each bid,* of the probable holding of each player. The assessment process continues non stop until the hand is played out.

It is not necessary to play bridge or fully understand the game to realize that bridge is a very complicated game that requires a great deal of knowledge and concentration for a person to master it. There is so much to remember that internalization is always a problem. Moreover, even as more and more becomes internalized, good players must still concentrate on those things that can never be internalized because they change with every hand. This explains why bridge is regarded by many as the most challenging card game ever, and why it is so very hard to become good at it.

What becomes clear from our own life experience is that the more things one needs to internalize in order to incorporate a particular behavior into one's beliefs and attitudes, the harder that process becomes.

The Bibace Theory requires internalizing the following two major principles:

1. We all have 'two brains', only one of which we control, and they are often in conflict.

2. All good human relationships are dependent on one person making the other feel good about himself and/or to avoid feeling bad about oneself.

With only two main ideas to keep in mind, the internalization process is reduced to a minimum, thereby maximizing the chances of success.

Rule #15 – Internalization of the principle of making others feel good about themselves is vital to good relationships, and conscious repetition is the key.

PART II-Applying the Theory

Chapter Eleven

Types of Relationships

Making others feels good about themselves is at the heart of all good relationships, and applies to all relationships. However, the specific *application* of the theory will differ somewhat from one kind of relationship to another. Let's examine the kinds of relationships and the different ways of dealing with them.

Relationships:

You and your Spouse **-** This is by far the hardest relationship to keep in good shape. It is usually the most important in couples' lives and provides each spouse with a great deal of power over the well being of the other.

You and your Family **-** Next to the spousal relationships, good family relationships are hardest to maintain. As the saying goes, "*You can choose your friends but not your family.*" Therefore, you must do your best to get along with them. With family, you have a history. Family relationships can often be intense and are often unavoidable because of that history. That is why interaction with family can be so troublesome.

You and your co-workers – These relationships are usually more limited in intensity. They are also often subject to a greater degree of choice, because you can often pick the kind of work you want. That means you can choose work in which interpersonal relationships are very important like selling or dealing with the public. Or you may choose work in which interpersonal relationships are few and far between, such as long-haul trucking, or inventory control.

Your social life is usually the easiest. Until you get married, you can choose all your own friends. After marriage, a degree of compromise is often required. As a result, you may be obligated to socialize with people your spouse does not particularly care for, or vice versa. However, even then the amount of time spent with people one regards as less desirable is limited.

Source of potential for good or bad relationships - Intensity and importance

The relationships that can have a significant impact on our lives are either intense or important or both.

Intense, in this context, means an unavoidable relationship in which the parties are deeply involved in each other's lives. They may often also be in each other's physical presence for a big part of their daily lives. The best examples are spouses and/or members of a family living together.

Importance, in this context, means the degree to which one person is dependent on a good relationship with another to achieve his own goals. The principle here is that the higher the degree of dependence, the greater the importance to the dependent person.

For example, a young child is totally dependent on his parents for all the things he needs and wants. Therefore, the child's relationship with his parents is extremely important.

Similarly, an employee is usually very dependent on his direct supervisor for his advancement, and so his relationship with that person is very important. The level of importance of one person to another can vary with time and circumstances.

For example, in early life, a parent's importance to a child is at its highest level for anybody. After the formative years, when the child has grown to adulthood, that level of importance will diminish, and will be replaced by the now adult child's spouse and own children.

Sometimes, the feeling of well-being can occur simply because one has met and been acknowledged by a very important person (VIP), like a rock star, sports star, movie star, or very well known or wealthy person.

That is why so many people will tend to tell others of the names of celebrities they happened to know or go to school with, before they became celebrities. Speaking casually of such acquaintances gives them a vicarious feeling of importance. It makes them feel good about themselves.

The Farghaly Pasha incident

I recall an incident when I was thirteen years-old that illustrates the point. I was born in Egypt of well off, French speaking, Sephardic Jewish parents. My father was the least important of a handful of cotton exporters in Egypt, at a time when "Cotton was King" and cotton exporters were regarded as the elite among businessmen. One particular man, Farghaly Pasha, was the number one cotton exporter in Egypt, as well as one of the richest men in the country. He was also a Pasha. The term Pasha was a title of nobility at the time of the Farouk monarchy, second in importance only to the King himself.

My father had occasion to take me to one of the cotton exporter association functions and introduced me to Farghaly Pasha. To me, at the time, meeting Farghaly Pasha was the equivalent of an American thirteen-year-old meeting Bill Gates or Mickey Mantle in his heyday.

When I reached out to shake Farghaly Pasha's hand, he took my hand in both of his and held it there for a few moments while he spoke to me. The effect on me was dramatic and never forgotten.

This great man had not merely met me and acknowledged me by shaking my hand, but had held my hand in both of his as he spoke kindly to me. It made me feel very good about myself as one worthy of being so "honored" by such a great man. This incident, which occurred over 60 years ago, is still fresh in my mind.

The "knowing a famous man" incident

Another interesting example involved my first client in the real estate brokerage business. This client was a member of one of the wealthiest families in the world. His name was Peter and he and I became friends. He was twenty-six when I met him.

One day he told me about how a particular small newsstand owner gushed over his father every time he saw him in the store. He wondered why anybody would fuss so much when the most the storekeeper could hope to gain financially from his father was the sale of a few dollars of magazines or candies.

What he did not see, but I was able to point out, was that to a man owning a small store, merely being able to say he knew Peter's father was a very big thing and made him feel very important and very good about himself, and about which he could proudly boast by "name dropping" the famous name among his friends.

The making a famous man laugh incident

My uncle, Joseph, was born and raised in Egypt at a time when the measure of a man was by and large how rich he was. The net worth of individuals and their relative wealth was a matter generally known and often discussed. In Egypt, the richer you were, the higher your society grade. There is more than a little truth to that statement everywhere in the world. Knowing such men – being able to "name drop" about such men – was a vicarious way for less rich individuals to feel good about themselves.

One day my uncle and I were driving one of the richest men in the world to his office. That man was, among other things, one of the major shareholders of an extremely profitable liquor company. I was twenty years-old at the time. There was a French joke I liked that bore repeating, particularly I thought to this liquor "king".

It seems that in a French bar a temperance group had posted a sign above the bar stating, "*Alcohol kills slowly*" under which a fellow with a sense of humor had added, "*We don't care, we are in no hurry!*" The joke got a good laugh from everybody in the car.

Later, my uncle, very impressed, said to me, "*You did very well. You made the great man laugh!*" It made my uncle feel very good about himself to have a young nephew who was able to make such a famous man laugh heartily at a joke related to the heart of his business. I felt pretty good about myself too.

The Family sub classifications: *Spouses, parent-to-child, child-to-parent, siblings, and other family relationships are described as follows:*

***Spouses* -** Spousal relationships are the most important, intense, and usually most difficult relationships. Spouses live together, eat together, sleep together, make love together, socialize together, parent together, suffer the ups and downs of life together, and sometimes even work together. It is also virtually impossible for them to avoid each other's presence (although some try their best).

Spouses also exercise considerable power over each other's ability to feel good about themselves. For a marriage to work, and good relationships to prevail between spouses, each has to agree with the other (or at least agree to disagree without being disagreeable), on more issues than with any other single person.

Moreover, they have to do it over a lifetime, and in spite of having their own lives become more difficult and complicated with the arrival of children with their own sets of needs and demands. It is no wonder that over half the people who get married in the USA wind up divorcing.

***Parent and child* -** There is no more important relationship to a child than his parent. The child is initially totally dependent on his parents for the satisfaction of all of his needs. Moreover, the relationship is both intense and important to both the parent and the child. To the child, the importance and power of the parent cannot be overemphasized.

The parent literally has the power (even if not the right), of life and death over the child. The parent has the power not merely to make the child happy and secure in his childhood and teen years, but also, and critically importantly, to provide the child with the emotional capital that will serve him well through life.

To most parents, there is nothing more important than seeing their child happy and successful. Achieving that goal is one of the things that can be the most effective in making the parents feel good about themselves.

Siblings - Relationships with siblings are second in intensity and importance to a child only to the relationships with his parents. One sibling's power over another is limited and a function of age and gender. Older and/or stronger siblings will be able to exercise some degree of power, often giving the advantage to boys who are generally physically stronger than their sisters.

The intensity will be dependent on the particular age differences and genders. The closer the age and gender the closer the relationship. For example, identical twins of either sex usually get along very well together and are often extremely important to each other all their lives.

Other family relationships - The first line relationships outside the nuclear family of parents and children include grandparents, aunts and uncles, and cousins. The intensity and importance of these relationships often varies from culture-to-culture and from family-to-family.

In some cultures, extended families are common. In these cultures, nuclear families can be, and often are, intensely involved with their extended families. Even in the USA these situations sometimes exist. Wherever these conditions exist, certain family members can take on a much greater degree of importance in each other's lives than would be expected otherwise.

However, in the USA, most extended families do not live in close proximity to each other. As a result, contact is limited between members of the nuclear family and others and so is the positive or negative potential impact of any relationship.

Work sub classifications: *Employer-to-employee, employee-to-employee, employer or employee-to-customer, employer or employee-to-vendor*

Employer to employee **-** In work relationships, just as in family relationships, some are more important than others. The importance of relationships will vary with the relative position of one individual to another. To the employee, the employer has a position of importance and power, not unlike a parent to a child.

The employee must maintain the best relationship he can with his boss and/or his direct supervisor. Because he is dependent on that person for advancement, favorable reviews, raises, and sometimes, and to some degree, working conditions.

Of course, a good employer knows the value of keeping his employees happy. He therefore also knows the importance of maintaining good relationships with all of them. The difference is one of degree. The employer is rarely dependent on any single employee for the success of his enterprise.

Employee-to-employee **-** The relationship here is similar to that of siblings in a family relationship. If the employees are on the same level, neither has any real power over the fate of the other.

Employer or employee-to-customer **-** The adage, *"The customer is always right"* is not a statement of fact. Rather, it is a statement advocating an attitude. That attitude is that regardless of how wrong the customer may be a good employer/employee will treat the customer *as if he is right.*

Doing that makes the customer feel good about himself, because most of us would like to be right all the time. No business can survive without satisfied customers. Therefore, in both intensity and importance, customers rank as the most important people to a business.

Every business deals intensely with customers daily and constantly. Customers are the lifeblood of a business and therefore their importance cannot be overstated.

***Employer or employee-to-vendor* -** To the vendor, the employer/employee of the enterprise he is attempting to sell is the customer. That creates for the Vendor the same position in terms of intensity and importance for him as is his buyer's customers are to him.

Social sub classifications - Social relationships include one's own friends and the friends of one's spouse or significant other. The level of intensity here is often up to the individual and how involved they care to be.

One can usually choose to see or not see friends as often as is mutually desired. Relationships are easiest when all parties to a relationship are involved with each other to the degree they choose and because they so choose.

In situations when one is involved with friends of one's spouse or significant other, one may find oneself around some people for whom one may not care. On these occasions a greater awareness of what is needed to maintain a good relationship will be needed.

Chapter Twelve

Application to Couples

Let us now take a more detailed look at relationships between couples. The word "couples," in this context, means two people living together in a formal or informal marital relationship. This definition includes the traditional heterosexual marital relationship as well as marriage between same sex partners.

The reasons why good couple relationships are so hard to maintain is because the more intensely involved two people are, the harder it is to avoid and/or resolve conflicts and enjoy the benefits of a good relationship.

In order to have a good relationship, couples have to get along and make mutually acceptable decisions in many areas. Two of these areas, sex and money are the two major causes of divorce in the USA.

Other areas are religion; having and rearing children; sharing of income producing and homemaking tasks; where to live; where and when to vacation; with whom to socialize; personal habits; and the kind and intensity of relationships with each other's families.

The list is much longer than comparable lists for any other kind of relationship, and therefore so much harder to make work. A great deal of television comedy is based on the difficulties couple face attempting to reconcile their views in all these areas.

Marriage is not a 50/50 proposition

Let's first look at two general considerations that particularly impact couples. First is the erroneous concept that marriage is a 50/50 proposition. Second is the personal general status or mood of each person at any particular time.

A successful marriage is NOT a 50/50 proposition. It is more of an 80/80 proposition.

Many people say, "Marriage is a 50/50 proposition." The idea is that each party needs to give 50% in order to make a marriage work. That suggests that the 50/50 rule means an equal number of compromises must be made in a marriage. That proposition, which first appears fair and reasonable, ***generally does not work***. That is because it does not factor in the personal, general status or mood of each individual at particular times.

The personal, general status of an individual is how that individual feels about himself at any particular time or what can be termed his "general mood." That feeling is often critical to a person's willingness and/or ability to compromise when it is his or her turn. It is short-term and can sometimes vary widely from the usual sense of self-worth. That feeling can often exercise some degree of positive or negative control over the individual.

It will be affected by a number of factors. These factors include general health, fatigue levels, satisfaction levels from immediate success or failure in particular endeavors, and more particularly the kind of very tough recession-type economic conditions that happen to be present at the time of this writing.

If one thinks of one's personal, general status on a 1-10 scale, one can think of the highest or euphoric state as being a 10 (say winning a major lottery, or graduating at the top of one's class, or receiving a national award). The lowest level or a 1 would be a state of clinical depression. We can think of most people operating at the middle level or at a five.

At that level, they are where they hopefully usually are in their lives. They are functioning reasonably well, with a reasonable level of self-esteem and a stress level that they can handle. When each member of the couple is at a five, then the 50/50 concept can work well, because the spirit of compromise essential to good relations in a marital situation is alive and well.

The where to go on vacation issue

Let us take an example in which the wife likes to vacation at the beach and the husband at the mountains. The couple agrees to go to the beach one year and the mountains the next. Or say they agree to celebrate Thanksgiving alternately at each other's parent's homes. But what if one or the other person is going through a rough patch and his or her general, personal mood/status falls to a three.

Gone, in the short-term, are compromise, reason, and rationale. Gone is the healthy spirit of intelligent cooperation. So what happens then? If the agreement is 50/50, it is possible that the party short-changed will rebel, because it is not "fair". The next thing may well be the refusal by the aggrieved party to go along with other 50/50 compromises. That can put the couple on the slippery slope of extended conflict and perhaps worse.

Not to mention that sometimes the distaste for a particular compromise may be much greater in one person than the other. For example, if one person loves the beach and doesn't mind the mountains, while the other hates the beach but is crazy about the mountains, the compromise of alternating vacations between the two will not work well. The solution may have to be two or even three vacations at the mountains for each vacation at the beach.

That is why the approach needs to be the 80/80 approach, with each person willing to compromise 80% of the time. In practice, of course, the result will approach the 50/50 standard as long as the parties are reasonably close to or above the 'number 5' level of general mood.

With this in mind, how does one apply the Bibace theory to couples' situations? There are five steps. The first four steps apply to all relationships and have been described earlier.

Here is Step Five: In couples, each person needs to recognize that his or her importance in the other person's life is very high and should receive very special attention. Family and the marital relationship is the basis of all civilization. It is therefore either *the* most important or at least equally important to any other, such as the child/parent in the early years. It goes without saying that whatever one has been doing that works well, one should continue to do.

Situations – The general mood and the specific situation

The General Mood - Every relationship, and particularly that of couples, involves two distinct parts. The first is what the French call "the atmosphere." The atmosphere or mood is the general prevailing emotional tone or general attitude that exists between the parties.

It is created by how they feel about each other, how each makes the other feel about him/herself, and generally how well they get along. The specific situation refers to a particular conflict that has arisen and how best to handle it.

<u>*The 'Odd Couple' mood*</u>

An excellent example of a very bad general mood was demonstrated in Neil Simon's smash hit *The Odd Couple.* In it two divorced men, Oscar and Felix, are living together for a mere three weeks. Oscar is extremely messy and Felix is compulsively neat. Felix is constantly getting on Oscar's nerves by compulsively cleaning, and complaining about Oscar's bad habits.

When the blowout occurs, Oscar complains about the constant nagging he is getting from Felix. Then, and critically important to the plot he adds, "*Even if you don't say a word, it doesn't help because I am expecting you to say something.*"

Thus, even temporary relief from a bad situation may not help to improve the mood/atmosphere because the *expectation* of unfavorable treatment is enough to create the same problem.

Often the behavior does not have to be spoken. A perceived look, a general attitude, or a gesture of impatience can suffice. It is obvious that the better the general atmosphere, the fewer specific problems will arise, and the more easily they will be resolved.

Techniques for boosting your partner's self-esteem and thus creating a good mood/atmosphere

First and foremost always be sincere. Insincerity will be detected and will be counterproductive.

Every couple does for each other. In an old fashioned traditional relationship, the male partner's job was bringing home the bacon, while the female partner's main job was taking care of the house and bringing up the children. It is likely that overlapping will occur in any good relationship. There will be even more so in modern relationships where both partners often work outside the home.

Each person should make a point of showing regular hearty appreciation for the other's contribution, even though that person's contribution is normal and expected.

For example, each should appreciate the efforts of the other in preparing a meal, or by expressing thanks after eating. The same expression of gratitude should prevail often with regard to keeping the house clean, the laundry done, the bills paid, and all the other chores that living together entails.

Express particular gratitude for any special effort your partner may have made to please you. *Keep bringing her flowers and make her feel like a Queen. Keep telling him he is wonderful and is still your King!*

Determine what your partner is or does that is important to him/her and seek to compliment your partner sincerely on that. The 'wrong' compliment can backfire. For example complimenting an intelligent and very sexy looking woman on her body might be viewed as insulting by her, because what is important to her is her intelligence.

A compliment on her 'sexy body' might be viewed as seeing her as a 'sex object' rather than an intelligent life companion! Give sincere compliments that recognize what's important to your partner.

The idea of "water tight compartments" in making your spouse feel good about her/himself

There are many wealthy men who believe that because they are taking excellent financial care of their wives their job is done! Their attitude can be summarized as follows: *I give her everything! She lives like a queen! She has jewelry, a beautiful car, a lovely house, two beautiful kids – yet she still complains. What more does she want?*

At less affluent levels, a similar attitude sometimes prevails. Then the husband may say: *I work hard to give her a nice home and to put food on the table. I don't drink or fool around. I'm a good parent and I take her on nice vacations! What more does she want?*

The reason the wives in these example are "not happy" is very simple. Making one's wife (or husband) "feel good about him/herself" can only be achieved by a proper balance of the fulfillment of both material and emotional needs.

The needs can be thought of as "water tight compartments", *each of which needs to receive a minimum level of fulfillment*. Because these compartments are 'water tight', overfilling one will still leave any other completely 'dry' or empty. The basic compartments are material and emotional. The material compartment can be thought of as first including survival needs and then including whatever level of material comfort one's society and peers regard as appropriate. The emotional compartment is filled by making the other person feel good about herself in whatever ways are appropriate in the circumstances.

The concept is easy to understand if we think of the most basic need of all human beings which is survival. To survive we need a minimum amount of each of four separate things: Food, water, shelter and security.

If we have ten times the food we need, but no water, we die. If we have all the water we need, but no food, we die. If we are in the jungle with all the food and water we need, but no shelter or security, we will probably also die. Thus survival requires that we have at least a minimum of all four essential elements.

As Shakespeare's King Richard III said as he lay unhorsed on the battlefield*: A horse, a horse, my kingdom* *for a horse!* He was willing to give up his crown for a single horse he needed for survival.

So it is for the survival of a solid relationship. Each spouse seeks to feel good about him/herself. In order for that to occur the other spouse must provide not merely a minimum level of acceptable financial stability, but a sense that he/she loves her/his spouse. Failure to do that will result in a failed relationship, because the 'water tight compartment of emotional need' cannot be filled by overflowing the 'water tight compartment of material need'.

Of course the opposite is also true. Overfilling the emotional need 'compartment' and failing to provide a minimum of material or financial support will not work either. The artistic soul who more than fills his loved one's emotional needs with poetry, affection, kind words and loving attention, will not be able to sustain a relationship in which he is unable to put food on the table, or a roof over his loved one's head.

Although many needs are universal, some particular needs may vary from person to person. The wise spouse will make sure these needs are identified and filled.

For example, if one spouse likes to attend a house of worship while the other doesn't, it would be wise for the less religious spouse to occasionally accommodate the other. Or if one spouse places particular importance on the celebration of certain days but the other doesn't, it would be wise to provide accommodation here too.

The bottom line is that the goal of making the other person feel good about him/herself cannot be fully achieved unless each of those things that are important to the other person are adequately addressed.

Techniques for special situations

The techniques suggested will work best when the general atmosphere or prevailing feeling is positive. However, they can also work at other times to address any immediate problem, while also improving the general mood/atmosphere.

There are two things to always keep in mind. The first is that the other person also has two separate parts of the brain, and may not be in full control of the emotional part. The second is that the immediate ability of the other person to control his or her own Beast is often dependant upon the kind of day he or she is having and his/her own general, personal mood/status.

The more one understands and remembers these two very important matters, the less likely one is to take offense at offensive behavior and therefore the more one can control one's own Beast and say and do the right thing.

The next thing to remember is the perennial task of giving your partner reasons to feel good about him or herself.

The worried husband and harried wife

Let's look at an example. The economy is bad. Sam is trying to do what he can to keep his job and pay the bills. He had to work late. Sam hoped to come home to enjoy a good dinner and some quiet time later. He comes home late for dinner. He finds his wife, Ann, having trouble with their two children. She is trying to put one to bed while trying to get the second to do his homework. She has not had time to make dinner and the house looks like a hurricane hit it because the kids were a little wild.

She snaps at him, *"You're an hour late for dinner. I needed you here on time to help with the kids. You never help. You expect me to do it all. They are your kids too, you know! You need to be a father every now and again. I can't do it all by myself! Now you're here, get your son to finish his homework while I finish putting your daughter to bed!"*

The natural reaction–Sam is thinking, *"Do I need this? Is it not bad enough that I have to fight with customers in a bad economy who want everything for nothing? That I don't know from one week to the next whether I'll still have a job, or whether my company will still be solvent or even in business? That I am in debt up to my eyeballs and may have to declare bankruptcy before long? Do I also have to come home to a messy house and a wife screaming at me because she can't do her job? And why does she have to say YOUR son and YOUR daughter when they are both OUR children?"*

In such a scenario, Sam's Beast is likely to take over his Logical Me and snap back in anger with some choice and unpleasant thoughts of his own. If that happens, the result will be a fight, a worsening of the atmosphere, and a continuing deterioration of the marital relationship; all of which will impact the children in a very negative way.

The recommended reaction and how to achieve it, before arriving home, the husband needs to be thinking, "*Times are tough for all of us. When times are tough, there is extra pressure on my wife and children as well as myself. I have to remember that both my wife and I are likely to have our Beasts take over and make trouble.*

Therefore, if my wife becomes upset and irritated over anything and attacks me, I need to remember that it is her Beast talking. That she cannot control that in herself. It is therefore up to me to defuse any disagreeable situation that may occur. I can only try to control my own reactions. By understanding what is going on I can supply my own Beast with feeling good about the self-satisfaction it is forever seeking. That is because <u>this very realization</u> is evidence *of intelligent insight that increases my Beast's self-esteem because it shows me how smart I am. That will allow me to react positively."*

The recommended dialogue by Sam: (Always speaking the truth sincerely)

"Sorry I'm late." (No mention of his very good reason for being late).

"I can see the kids gave you a very rough time tonight." (No mention of the messy house or the wife's emphasis on YOUR kids)

"I know how busy you are and how tough the kids can be." (No mention of YOUR kids or even OUR kids, only THE kids, lest anything else be viewed as an insulting response)

"I'll help John finish his homework and don't worry about dinner. I'll help you with that later."

This reaction will at least defuse the situation, reduce or eliminate the chances of the situation escalating into a lot worse, and perhaps bring the wife around to where she, too, may recognize her unreasonable behavior.

Chapter Thirteen

You and... You and your child

<u>*A supremely important relationship for the child*</u>

There is no more important relationship to a child than the relationship he has with his parents. Every parent must realize that the parent/child relationship is one of enormous power for the parent. In extreme cases, that power can result in the actual death of the child through neglect and/or abuse. In lesser cases, it can result in the belief that the parent can and will kill the child in the event that the child does not behave as instructed. That perception can produce terrible adverse long-term consequences in feelings of self-esteem and the ability to do well.

The comedian, Bill Cosby, once said to his sitcom son, *"I brought you into this world and I can take you out."* That sounded funny to the audience. But if the son believed his father, it might have scarred him for life.

Your power over your child for good is also very great. Nobody's approval is more important to a child than that of his parents. Even in later life an adult will compare his own success in life to that of his father, as opposed to a societal standard.

The comparison to "Daddy"

I had a friend who was a very wealthy man, a graduate of an Ivy League College, and a star athlete on his college ice hockey team. Yet, in spite of these achievements, he still *regarded himself as a failure* because he inherited his initial very substantial fortune from his father. He felt that way even though he had successfully multiplied his original inheritance twenty-fold by his own efforts. Compared to his father, he felt he was a failure.

At the same time, I knew another young man, Mike. Mike's father had come to Canada as a young man. He had remained an illiterate day laborer all his life and never learned English. Yet Mike, obviously far less successful in absolute terms than my other friend, *regarded himself as a great success.*

That was because he had reached what he regarded as the elite status of being a union electrician making union pay. Therefore, compared to his father he was a great success. The fact that one man was earning millions of dollars a year as a result of his own efforts and the other was earning a few hundred dollars a week did not change how either saw himself.

This illustrates how critical the parent relationship is to creating in the child whatever sense of self-worth and self-esteem he will probably carry for the rest of his life. That relationship will determine how well the child will interact with others, and how successful he is likely to be, as well as how happy that child is likely to become.

In turn, that relationship will mold the child in ways that will either help or hinder the eventual upbringing of the child's own children. In extreme cases, it may be a major factor in determining whether the child grows up to be a good citizen and a contributing member of society, or a criminal who survives by stealing or hurting others, and who will spend much of his life in prison.

Every parent has the very important job of contributing to his/her child's self-esteem. This is a role that should not be taken lightly and the marital status of a parent does not change the parental role. It does, however, become more difficult and complicated if the parents are separated or divorced.

A child's self-esteem is lessened when the child witnesses his parents argue or if the child feels the parents' unhappiness is in some way his fault. In such cases, special care should be taken to make sure the child feels no guilt concerning the parents' failed relationship.

On "pushing" children constantly

Some parents believe that the best approach to helping their child do well is to keep pushing the child continually to do better. Thus, if a child gets an "A," he is asked why it is not an "A+." If he makes the high school team in a particular activity but isn't the star, the parent will still sound dissatisfied.

Encouraging the child to do better within the child's limitations is good, but only if the child is made to feel good about his accomplishments along the way.

As a hyperactive child, a great deal of the time I was told I was no good by my family and many teachers. I was constantly made to feel badly about myself. Only a very strong personality saved me from believing what I was told and becoming what I had been labeled. That is why, the level of achievement should not be as important as the level of effort shown by the child.

Parents and children are locked into their relationships for life. Neither party can change that. The *intensity* of the relationship, as measured by the amount of contact between the parties, may differ from one family to another, but it will usually remain high until the child reaches maturity.

The *intensity* of the relationship will diminish over time as the child matures, goes off to college, and eventually leaves the home for good to make it on his own. However, the *importance* of the relationship can and should always remain of the first order.

The general mood

As in all relationships the first aspect to consider when dealing with your child is the general mood/atmosphere. The quality of the atmosphere or prevailing feeling in the home, and therefore between the parties, can vary greatly.

That quality can range from the highest and best in a two parent, loving home with supportive, understanding, and involved parents, to the worst. In which case, the parents may be abusive, unloving, unsupportive, and unable to supply even minimal levels of financial security, proper health care or decent shelter, to name a few of the issues involved.

Ideally, every child should have two loving parents and a stable, secure, healthy, and happy environment in which to grow. The absence of any of these factors will create an atmosphere that is harder to keep positive.

For example, all other things being equal, every single parent home faces greater challenges than a two parent home. Other factors such as the loss of a job by a parent, or a parent who drinks excessively, etc., will also make things more difficult.

Techniques for making one's child feel good about him or herself and thus creating a good atmosphere

One should always be sincere. There is, however, a somewhat different approach in the concept of sincerity when dealing with children. One can be sincere when praising a child's efforts, even if the outcome is not praiseworthy per se. What an adult might regard as insincere flattery, a child will appreciate as welcome encouragement.

Thus, if the child's work *represents improvement,* whether in effort or attitude, though not in outcome, sincere praise for the improvement is still warranted. It is only if a child is able but refuses to make any effort to even try to improve that praise should be withheld.

Children often have household chores to do. Express gratitude to them for doing chores as requested. Express particular gratitude for any special effort your child may have made to please you.

Determine what your child does that is important to him and seek to compliment your child sincerely on that. We all teach our children to use the "magic" words please and thank you. We should always remember to use them ourselves with our children.

Techniques for special situations

The techniques suggested will work best when the general mood or prevailing feeling is positive. However, they can also work to not only address the immediate problem, but also to improve the general atmosphere.

There are two things to remember at all times. The first is that *like you and everybody else,* the other person is not always in control of his or her emotions.

The second is that the immediate ability of the other person to exercise control over his or her own Beast depends on the kind of day he or she is having and his/her own general, personal mood.

The point is that the more one becomes aware of these two vital considerations, the more likely one is not to *take offense at offensive behavior,* and the more one remains in control of one's own Beast. Therefore, the more one is likely to say and do the right thing.

Help in changing "rebel's" minds – Michael's epiphany

The following example involves a close friend's son, Michael, a twenty-two-year old who is a tall, muscular, athletic, good looking, very bright and multi-talented artist who composes music and plays an excellent guitar. He is also a very good musical actor and he also paints. Michael was getting top grades at a very good art school, but decided to quit after two years because *"the school had nothing to teach him any more."*

He was rebellious, worked only occasionally, and always sought all the financial help he could get from his parents. He regarded his parents as having an absolute obligation to support him. Neither parent was in a position to do so, even if they were inclined to enable an artist to continue in his anti-social behavior.

He was often very rude to both his parents, insisting that he alone understood life because he was an artist, and only an artist could really appreciate life. He further asserted that all "non-artists" were not really fully alive or "with it." Therefore, he could not be understood by such "ignorant people".

The usual interaction would commence with some derogatory remark made by Michael to his mother about how ignorant she was about artistic matters or some such issue. She would always respond in anger and with some rational argument about the fact that all this artistic talent and interest did not feed, house, or clothe the artist.

She would add that she was struggling financially, herself, and helping him financially was a continuing strain she could not sustain indefinitely, all of which was true.

But the more she presented logical arguments, the more stubborn he became in talking about artistic integrity and the need for her to understand and support his lifestyle as a true artist. Thus, the battle between the immoveable object and the irresistible force continued.

Going with the flow

I took a different approach. Instead of fighting his concept, I "went with the flow" of his position and brought his mom on board. I said and his mom agreed, "Okay, I am not an artist, but I will not argue with your logic. From where you sit, I can certainly understand why you take that view."

Let's now examine the logical consequences of that action. The moment that his mom and I stopped fighting him he no longer had any opponents to fight. That forced him to start looking at the consequences of his decisions. In terms of my theory, this is what happened:

His Beast, in a desire to *feel good* because *he felt bad about himself*, sought solace in verbal abuse[40]. He did that by attacking his mom and dad and blaming them for his lack of financial resources and their failure to understand the soul of an artist.

The verbal abuse of his parents was Michael's *feel good* substitute for the *feeling good about himself* he lacked as a college dropout and an unemployed, penniless artist.

However, once the ***resistance*** to the verbal abuse disappeared, there was no battle left to win. He was then forced to listen to the consequences of his decisions. One can't keep arguing with someone who agrees with you.

[40] Verbal abuse being *'bad source feel good'*

That was when I was able to discuss these consequences very calmly and non judgmentally, saying that I understood the following, all of which was completely true:

- *He was free to make whatever decisions he wanted.*
- *He was a very bright and talented man (which certainly helped).*
- *Although his mother and I might disagree with his decisions, we accepted the fact that he was entitled to make them and live with the consequences, all of which made him feel good about himself. That brought him around to at least opening his mind to listening to what I had to say, which brought us to the consequences of his proposed actions.*
- *I pointed out to him that as an artist who had already done very well in two years of college, he could choose between the following: Going back to school and getting a degree from an accredited college in order to be able to get a job making a decent living teaching art. Or, he could try to survive from the sale of his art, which he knew to be a very difficult, if not impossible task.*

Though an accomplished guitarist and composer, he refused to use his musical talents to earn a living. He claimed he wrote music only for himself and would not play anyone else's music for pay.

So it became clear to him that he could go back to school and get the diploma he had spurned for its substance, but was necessary for its credibility in getting a job later. Alternatively, he could suffer the certainty of the indignity, poverty, and pain of a long-term inability to make a living as an artist.

I told him that neither his mother nor I could do more than point the way to what we believed were his best options and explain the alternatives. He could then examine what we said and satisfy himself in whatever way he wanted as to whether he agreed. *In any case, he could do as he saw fit.*

The process took many weeks of going over alternatives and discussions related to the issues. In the end, he made a 180 degree change in attitude. He became polite, loving, hard-working, and went back to college. He saw the light. He also fell in love with a charming young lady after he began to change his views. No doubt that must have helped make him see the wisdom of rational choices.

The catalyst and the question of gratitude

The contribution to Michael's change by his mother and me was a typical instance of what I call *"catalytic"* behavior. That is the changing of one's own behavior that indirectly results in changing the behavior of another. Without the change in our behavior there would almost certainly have been no change in Michael's.

If you go through that experience, you will probably find (as we did with Michael) that there is very often no realization by the person you helped of the 'catalytic' effect you contributed.

The recipient, as it were, of the benefits of your behavior (Michael in our true life example) sees *his own changes as only having occurred through his own good judgment and insights.*

Even a complete reversal of behavior, from very bad to very good in a person, is not likely to be attributed to help from others, but only to that person's own insight and intelligence.

What actually happened is that the Beast in Michael gave way to his Logical Me. Therefore, the perception by his Logical Me of the wisdom of the position suggested is seen by Michael as having been a personal discovery, not something for which anyone else should be given credit.

The reaction is not unlike a student getting straight A's in class. That student will very rarely attribute credit to his teachers, the quality of her books or the environment created by her school. Rather she will look upon herself as the only one either completely or almost completely responsible for the results.

The bottom line, however, is not only that this should not matter, but that the result is the best possible outcome. What is important is the excellent outcome, not who receives credit for it. It should be enough for those who are truly responsible for triggering the change, albeit catalytically, to know the truth and quietly enjoy the feeling good about oneself that accompanies that knowledge.

There is even a major advantage to the result. That is because the more a person feels that it is she and she alone who is responsible for changing her views, her attitudes, and her life, the better the chances are that the change will be permanent. Therefore, this result, though a little disappointing to the catalyst's ego, should be welcomed as the ultimate success.

What about Gratitude?

Jean Jacques Rousseau, the French philosopher said:

Gratitude is a duty which ought to be paid, but which none have a right to expect.

It is a very good thing to always show gratitude for all good things that one receives, even if that attitude is not particularly "normal" in life's usual activities. Showing sincere gratitude makes others feel good about themselves. It is also one of the major keys to keeping relationships solid.

On the other hand, *expecting gratitude* is quite another matter. Someone once said, "*If you are looking for gratitude, you will find it in the dictionary!*" The absence of gratitude is regrettably far more common than its presence. So it is wise to accept gratitude as something like the "quality of mercy" which falls like soft rain from heaven blessing the giver and the receiver. But it is unwise to *expect* gratitude.

Moreover, the absence of gratitude in circumstances described above in the "Michael metamorphosis" is the ultimate tribute to the "catalyst."

In the words of the 17th verse of the Tao Te Ching, whom legend tells us was written by Lao-tzu and is a Chinese philosophical, widely translated work[41] the true leader "... *speaks little. He never speaks carelessly. He works without self interest and leaves no trace. When all is finished, the people say, 'We did it ourselves.'*"

This is why the absence of gratitude, when a very good outcome has been achieved by the catalytic effect of one's efforts, can be seen as the ultimate tribute to one's efforts to help another.

An important word about divorced or separated couples and their children

Most divorces and many separations are bitter. Lawyers will testify that the bitterest disputes in court are between divorcing spouses. Long-term business partners follow second in the level of bitterness, and the least bitter are between strangers fighting over money. The reason is that the depth of hatred and anger in divorce and other disputes is proportional to the original depth of love and affection during the marriage or business partnership.

[41] The whole as printed in Dr. Wayne Dyer's *Change Your thoughts, Change Your Life,* Published by Hay House in 2007

Each spouse/partner feels a much greater degree of pain in a major dispute involving a person they loved and regard themselves as having done things for in every respect than they would feel from a stranger. As a result, each individual's Beast often feels a tremendous need to attack the other person. That need manifests itself in a number of ways.

One of the ways is by attempting to justify one's own reasons for divorcing by telling the whole world, including the children of the union, that the other spouse is to blame. The attacks on the spouse are often vicious and are based on the perception of the aggrieved spouse. That perception can never be more than the result of *subjective reality* and may or may not be at all true.

However, regardless of the validity of the attacks, it is critically important to do all one can to avoid negativity when dealing with the children. An attack by one parent on another *will virtually always also be experienced by the child as an attack on the child.* This is because the child thinks of himself as the product of *both* parents and wants very much to believe that he is a good person, *and therefore a product of good parents.*

Thus the less the child is made to think of either of his parents, *the less he will think of himself.* An attack by one parent on another will make the child feel badly about itself, which is the opposite of what every parent should want for their child.

The situation is similar to the fictional story of the *Corsican Brothers.* They were twins who shared the extraordinary characteristic that a blow on one brother *would only be felt by the other.* In our case, a verbal attack told to a child about his parent, although intended to fall only on that parent, actually falls principally on the child who hears it, not on the parent who is not there.

You and your parent

In this context, the word "child" refers to the full period of time from birth to the death of the child or parent. Obviously, the age and level of maturity of the child will control the degree to which the child will either want to or be able to understand the information offered here. Nevertheless, the general principles apply.

Love for a child should be present at birth. As soon as the child is old enough to understand, he or she should consciously become aware of a parent's love. This is true, whether or not the parent is able to properly show that love and whatever the lifestyle. Crack addicts in prison have been known to love and fight for children whose father they cannot even identify.

The child should also remember, if at all possible, that the parent is also subject to the two parts of the brain, and therefore not always able to control the emotional part. Thus, the child should seek to make the parent feel good about him/herself by performing as well as possible at school and obeying the parent as well as showing demonstrative love to the parent. When the child becomes an adult, the relationship will necessarily change.

You and the workplace

There are three kinds of relationships in the workplace: You and your superior; you and your subordinates; you and your peers.

The importance of the general atmosphere or mood

As in all relationships, the first thing to consider is the *general atmosphere*, which is the prevailing sentiment in the workplace. When the general atmosphere is good, and the employees are happy campers, proud of the company they work for, and satisfied with their work and pay, it is much easier for them to work harmoniously together.

Where the opposite prevails, and the staff feels unappreciated, abused by superiors, exploited by the employer, treated unfairly and in a discriminatory manner, it will be very difficult to get individual employees to self-motivate to do what is best for maintaining good relationships.

The responsibility for the creation and maintenance of that good, prevailing sentiment lies with management. Good companies know the importance of doing this. They also know that in order to do this a number of practices have to be put in place, *all of which will tend to make the employees happy because they will be made to feel good about themselves.*

Some of these practices include treating the employees fairly and in a non-discriminatory manner; referring to them as associates or team members as opposed to employees or clerks, or some other job description; praise and recognition for jobs well done, periodic employee reviews that are perceived as fair by the recipients, and the creation and maintenance of an esprit de corps or team spirit among the staff members.

A few aspects of a business will occasionally lie beyond the ability of management to maintain positive feelings among the staff. In severe recessions, it is hard to keep morale high among staff members who wonder if they will still be employed in the days to come. Nevertheless one should keep trying.

You and your subordinate

The superior or supervisor-to-subordinate relationship is very important. It is similar, but not as powerful as the parent-to-child relationship. Like the parent, the superior wields a great deal of power over the subordinate. Your subordinate is protected, to some extent, by laws and sometimes by company rules, which limit your power as his superior to be unfair or unreasonable. Still, even within those limits as a superior, you are in a position to do much good or harm to your subordinates.

Therefore, the first thing that you, as a superior, should recognize is the power you wield. Then you must decide to use it wisely. You should recognize that to the subordinate, you are one of the most important people in his life. Your subordinate's continued employment, working conditions, fair evaluation, potential advancement, career opportunities, and ability to choose vacation time may all depend on you.

As a good superior, you will want to get the best out of your subordinates in the best interests of both the enterprise and the subordinate. To do so, you must apply the same principles as in all good relationships. To wit: *Make the subordinate feel good about himself and keep in mind that the subordinate has two parts of his brain that are sometimes in conflict, only one of which he controls.*

Making the subordinate feel good about himself requires you to do the following:

Praise the subordinate often for work well done. Never think or verbalize, "*That's what you are being paid for,*" because that implies that good work is the norm and need not be recognized. Even if that is true, in real life it remains bad practice.

Some bosses avoid too much praise because they are afraid that will cause their employees to ask for more money.

What truth there may be to that is most often far outweighed by the positive feelings created. The more talented the subordinate, the higher the praise needed to be effective.

Some very talented executives are used to doing excellent work and used to being praised for it. Saying he or she merely did well, or even very well to such a person might be taken as insulting and 'damning by faint praise'. That would make the person feel bad rather than good about himself. To these kinds of people, recognition that their work is extraordinary is required, but only if it really is.

Here are the guidelines for making your subordinates feel good about themselves:

- *Give your subordinate full credit with your own boss for the work she does and particularly for whatever good ideas your subordinate originates.*
- *Treat your subordinate as a member of your team.*
- *Take a sincere interest in your subordinate's personal life.*
- *Get to know the names of his wife and children and learn who and what he is outside the workplace.*
- *Minimize the effect of her errors and the effect of your boss's opinion of him.*
- *Never attribute errors you make to your subordinate.*

You and your boss

Your position vis-à-vis your boss is similar, but not as weak as a child is to his parent[42]. Your boss holds much of your destiny, working conditions, advancement, potential career opportunities, fair treatment, and fair evaluation in his hands. He may or may not be a good or fair person. Nevertheless, he or she is the one with whom you must deal.

[42] You can change bosses but never parents.

As always, the principles remain the same. In order to create and maintain a good relationship with your boss, you must *sincerely make your boss feel good about himself, while keeping in mind that your boss, just like you, has two parts of the brain sometimes in conflict, only one of which he controls.* Let me suggest a word of caution. Many bosses expect a degree of insincere 'sucking up' from their subordinates. Insincerity is often anticipated, and therefore more carefully than ever to be avoided.

You and your colleagues (peers)

Colleague relationships are those between employees of equal rank and can vary from the easiest to the hardest of all relationships to keep intact. In such relationships, there is a natural sense of unity and alliance of interests. That is because as peers, your relationships are perceived as the "us" in any "us and them" perception.

This means that the relationships between peers are strengthened by a common interest in the well-being of their class. It is also strengthened by the bonding of working for the same enterprise. Moreover, contact between peers can vary from constant daily interaction to minimal daily contact.

For example, the members of a two or three man construction subcontractor crew on a construction site may require the men to be in constant contact and cooperation with each other, all day, every working day.

On the other hand, the supervisors of those crews may only be in minimal touch with other supervisors, perhaps early in the morning and sometimes at the end of the day. Clearly, the need for good relationships between peers working with each other all day will be harder to maintain than for supervisor peers who see each other rarely and do not necessarily have any direct job obligations to each other.

As always, the principles remain the same. In order to create and maintain a good relationship among peers, each must *make the other feel good about himself and not take personally times when emotions overtake logic when reacting to situations.*

Making one's peer feel good about himself requires the following:

- *Sincerely and often give praise for work well done.*
- *Treat the peer as a team member.*
- *Take a sincere interest in the peer's personal life. Get to know the names of his wife and children and learn who and what he is outside the workplace.*
- *Minimize the effect of your peers' errors and the effect of your boss's opinion of yourself and him that may result from his errors.*
- *Never attribute your errors to your peers.*
- *Always give all credit to your peers when credit is due.*

You and your friends

Until one acquires a significant other through marriage or otherwise, social relationships are the easiest of all to create and maintain. This is because as long as you remain unattached, you are the only one picking the people who are your friends and with whom you choose to socialize. Later in life when you develop significant other relationships, compromises are often necessary.

As long as we are not attached, we can pick all our own friends. We can see who we want, when we want, and do what we want with them. That makes good relationships easy. Friendships develop as a result of a commonality of interests, likes and dislikes, similarity of backgrounds, tastes in entertainment, leisure activities, philosophies of life, and so on. Here, there is a minimum need for the application of special relationship skills.

However, after we acquire a partner in life, the picture changes. Now we tend to socialize with couples. That brings up certain problems. One now has to socialize with the partner's friends at least part of the time. Problems can crop up when the partner's couple friends aren't as compatible with one as one's own friends. Of course, one can limit contact with other couples where there is an absence of compatibility among all the parties.

As with other relationships, the more each person in the relationship contributes to the self-esteem of others, the stronger the relationship will become.

You and your Romantic interests

In earlier chapters, we discussed the relationships between couples. Romantic interests are the relationships between two people who are seeking significant others in their lives. The two people may be of the opposite sex or the same sex. The relationship may be one of marriage, living together, or some other form of long-term partnership involving intimacy. Books have been written and web sites exist purporting to help people make appropriate life partner choices. There is already much known on the subject and plenty of good advice available.

For example, it is well known that one of the most important reasons for successful relationships between couples is shared values. Web sites offer a number of tests that one can take and questions that one can ask of a candidate to determine the level of shared values to determine potential compatibility between two people.

However, what is not discussed is one key piece of information, which is the degree of control that each person has over his own Beast. The reason is the apparent lack of significant knowledge regarding the power of the Beast over a person's behavior. The degree of that may be somewhat measurable.

We have seen how the Beast, just like the Logical Me is forever seeking to feel good about itself. We have also seen that the *more* emotional currency received the *less* the need and tendency of the Beast to substitute feeling good for feeling good about itself. Conversely, the less such emotional currency received, the greater the tendency of the Beast to indulge in destructive activities.

Therefore, a person who has had a harsh and unhappy childhood is going to be more likely to react inappropriately in all later relationships. It is also probable that the degree of unhappiness in a child's early years will more or less track the degree of inappropriateness of his behavior as an adult.

This information, alone, should not be the only consideration when choosing a partner. It should, however, add a potentially significant tool to one's search criteria. Obtaining this information may or may not be easy. General questions about a candidate's early life may offer a clue. Questions about current relationships and the reasons for the possible failure of earlier relationships may also provide useful clues.

Feeling lucky to be with you

If you feel lucky to be with somebody, there will be a natural tendency on your part to say and do things that indicate the fact and therefore will make the other person feel good about him/herself. I recall one significant other in my life often saying on the subject of our excellent relationship, "*How did I get so lucky?"* The statement made me feel very good about myself.

Of course, the relationship would not have gone very well if I, too, did not feel as she did and I did not return the gesture. The level of "feeling lucky" must be in balance. Otherwise, eventually, the partner who makes continual gestures to show their good fortune in being with the other could feel unwanted, unloved, or taken for granted after the "honeymoon" phase.

The Queen Bee

An experience I once had describes the absence of this feeling and the resulting collapse of the relationship. We had been dating for a very short while when she told me of a previous person whom she had stopped dating after a few weeks. She told me that he once said, "*I want you to know that you are dating a person of quality.*" To which she answered, "*Mister, I know quality, and you ain't it!*"

It occurred to me that such a woman had such a high opinion of herself that it was unlikely that she would ever feel *"lucky"* to be with anyone. Rather, she would likely feel that the other person should feel very lucky to be with her.

It seemed to me that she saw herself as the 'Queen Bee' in a kingdom of drones that should be happy to serve her. As a result, I called her to break off our budding relationship. I explained that I didn't think any relationship would work when one of the two would always feel it was only the other who was lucky to be in the relationship.

The lady called a few days later to say she had been thinking a great deal about our chat and still wanted to see me as a friend. Mistakenly thinking that her attitude had changed, I went along and we became an item.

She was always comfortable bringing a number of my shortcomings to my attention. I agreed with her about most of the things she said, but I would have preferred not to hear them from her.

Then, one evening over two large glasses of wine *(in vino veritas or wine speaks truth)* she hit me with a new triple whammy, none of which I agreed with, and which *made me really feel very bad abut myself.*

We had a date for later that week, and after reflecting on the overall situation, it became clear to me that her speech was a dumping speech, whether or not she fully realized it. I decided to call her to acknowledge it was over between us.

After several failed attempts to reach her on the phone, I left a message on a Friday informing her of my views and cancelling our dinner date for the next evening. She did get the message on Friday. It did not disturb her at all, because surprisingly she never called back until after our scheduled date on Saturday night.

Her very casual explanation was that she had expected me to <u>get over it</u>. I told her I wasn't over it, but *au contraire* felt it was over. I did offer to meet with her and explain my reasons. Initially, she was interested, but subsequently called back to say, "*Since you have clearly made up your mind, there is no point in meeting*," and we did not meet.

For many weeks and then even 18 months later she made repeated attempts to revive the relationship. None worked. Moreover, I believe her "Queen Bee" mind that had originally caused the problem, prevented her from doing what she could have done as her best bet to get what she wanted.

We communicated extensively after the break. Never once in all that time did she say anything like, "*I truly love you. I am terribly sorry. I will do anything to get back together with you. I should never have said what I said.*" The closest she was able to come to apologizing about the triple whammy was to say, "*I was joking when I said it.*"

I have known a few other Queen Bees, women who are indeed very attractive and talented and who should be able to find good relationships. But these women appear to have difficulty with any relationship in which their significant other is not awed with their talents and forever willing to play second fiddle to them.

A relationship built on one partner worshipping the other can virtually never be a very good long-term relationship. Each partner must be willing to accept the other with all of his or her faults and still feel lucky to be with her/him.

The King Macho

There are undoubtedly as many 'King Machos' who are the male equivalent of the Queen Bee, in the world as there are Queen Bees. A 'King Macho' would be a man probably blessed with very good looks and a great body and probably sufficient personal charm to attract many women. Such a man might also feel any woman with him should deem herself lucky, while he might never be likely to experience the same feeling.

Rule #16 – Positively and sincerely altering our own behavior is the catalyst that can and will often positively alter the behavior of others.

PART III-Broader Implications

Chapter Fourteen

Overview

The *Ronald Bibace Universal Theory of Human Behavior* may constitute a step forward in human knowledge that has substantial implications beyond those discussed. That is because learning more about what motivates all material human behavior should constitute an important step forward in many fields of human knowledge.

In general, changing one's own behavior for the better is an important goal. Helping others change their behavior for the better can be equally important. At the state level, schools and all levels of law enforcement might be able to help bullies as well as street and prison gangs reform their ways in non coercive ways. In the private area, businesses could profit from the application of the principles explained.

What controls our thoughts and behavior is a subject that impacts philosophy and metaphysics (the ultimate reality of things) as well as being of compelling interest to the disciplines of psychology and psychiatry, sociology and religion. Let us break down the different areas and the kind of potential progress that might be achieved:

Psychology and Psychiatry - If materially true, the ideas presented here may well constitute an important change in current thinking. A change in the therapeutic treatment of patients in troubled relationships by primarily stressing the importance of making others feel good about themselves could ensue.

The same process could increase their 'emotional intelligence' or their ability to deal with their own emotions and those of others. Such a result could provide substantial benefits to the patients and major savings in costs of treatments. Because the potential impact could be most important on the field of psychology the subject has been treated in Chapter Nineteen – *Why I wrote this book* along with the three appendices.

Romantic interests - Knowing the level of happiness and emotional capital accumulated by a potential romantic partner as a child could be very helpful in determining the likely level of control the romantic candidate has over his or her Beast. That information could be a good indication of the possibility of unreasonable or even abusive behavior. If and when such behavior surfaces, the same knowledge could help reduce or even eliminate it, or at the very least better cope with it.

Business interests - One of the biggest problems in accepting change in business are the obstacles created by the egos of the top people. Helping individuals overcome ego problems stemming from Beast/limbic brains that seek inappropriate satisfaction could do wonders for the bottom line.

State interests - The state is responsible for the Nation's defense, the maintenance of law and order and the education of its children from childhood through high school.

Defense: One particular problem in the defense of the Nation is that of terrorist suicide bombers and their recruitment. A better understanding of their motivation and rationale might well result in providing them with a better and less lethal substitute for their behavior, thereby reducing their threat to our Nation, while redirecting their energies to socially acceptable alternatives.

Law and Order: The 'Gang' Problem in and out of Prisons. One particular problem facing the state in maintaining law and order is the existence and power of street and prison gangs. These gangs have become so powerful that they constitute a very serious threat to law and order both in and out of prisons. The application of the principles in this book could provide a better understanding of their motivation and recruitment and subsequently a methodology for redirecting their energies away from criminal behavior.

Education: This country is currently coping with many serious problems in education. Among these problems is the quality of some of the public schools and the issue of bullying. It is a given that at least some of the Nation's public schools are failing to provide their students with the required level of skills to enable them to compete in a modern world. Moreover, many schools have to cope with the adverse consequences on education, peace of mind, and even physical harm to some students, arising from bullying.

Improving learning: There is strong anecdotal evidence to suggest that teaching students is easier and more effective when the students are made to feel good about themselves. The application of the principles in this book by teachers could therefore potentially significantly improve education in some situations.

Bullying: If indeed, as postulated here, bullies are seeking to feel good about themselves in destructive ways through the exercise of abusive physical and psychological power over weaker students, then the application of the principles in this book may well provide them with the substitute positive feelings through socially acceptable behavior.

Philosophy and Metaphysics –

Philosophy is a Greek word meaning "lover of wisdom." Every lover of wisdom is necessarily a seeker of knowledge. Increased knowledge about how man thinks and what motivates men would constitute a major interest and some advance in man's knowledge.

Metaphysics is defined as *the ultimate reality of things.* The greater the knowledge acquired about all things and particularly the workings of the brain, the closer we can get to the ultimate reality of things.

Religion – Religion is generally concerned with spiritual matters, saving souls, encouraging virtue and discouraging sin. God gave Moses the Ten Commandments. The Catholic religion has codified the Seven Deadly Sins and the Seven Heavenly Virtues. It could be of some interest to track some of the actions of the Logical me and the Beast within us see how and when they cope with "these rules to live by".

Sociology – Sociology is defined as: *The study of society, human social interaction, and the rules and processes that bind and separate people not only as individuals, but as members of associations, groups, and institutions*[43]. Sociology deals with the creation of groupings in society and what makes them cohesive. Basic human motivations are very much in play here too.

[43] (see en.wiktionary.org/wiki/sociology)

Chapter Fifteen

Business Interests at the Senior Management Level

As discussed, good relationships are essential to all successful businesses. We have seen what it takes for individuals at every business level to function optimally for themselves and the enterprise for which they work. In this section, we will address a particular matter regarded by many as a major problem.

The problem in question can sometimes mean the death knell of a company. That problem is the unwillingness and/or perhaps inability at top management levels to always recognize the winds of change occurring in their business, *notwithstanding clear evidence available and sometimes repeatedly brought to their attention.*

<u>Give it more time or do more of the same</u>

The scenario usually involves a business strategy that has been put in place by the Chief Executive Officer or CEO. The policy is not working and the manager in charge is unwilling to change it. Usually, the CEO will either argue that more time is needed to allow the policy to work or that more of the same is needed.

The most recent book on the subject is entitled *Denial: Why Business Leaders Fail to Look facts in the*

Face - and What to Do About it. (ISBN 978-1-59184-313-9). It is written by Richard S. Tedlow, Professor of Business Administration at Harvard Business School.

In page 204 of his excellent book Mr. Tedlow states:

Despite the best efforts of psychologists, sociologists and management consultants, denial will remain a pitfall of business life. To think that even the most persuasive advice, studies, or cautionary tales, can eliminate the all-too-human proclivity to shield oneself from bad news would itself be an exercise in denial. Mr. Tedlow's views are currently 100% correct and very much the norm that this book is respectfully challenging.

The argument being made by CEO's of failing businesses is that the policy is fundamentally sound but lacks time or sufficient resource commitment to succeed. This presents an argument that only time or more money can effectively refute, which is often something that the enterprise cannot afford.

The power of the CEO is sometimes near absolute. Even if it isn't, it is not easy for a Board of Directors to fire a CEO. Firing a high ranking employee presents potential, serious repercussions on employee morale, as well as adverse share value reaction from perceived lack of confidence in top management. In turn, the situation gives a misguided CEO considerable power to unwittingly destroy his company.

Let's examine what is happening. CEO's become CEO's as a result of being hard working men or women with a lot of confidence in themselves, and more often than not, considerable egos. They thrive and feel good about themselves on the basis of their success as top managers. That success is at least partly based on the success of the business strategies they either initiated or fully supported.

To most of these individuals, admitting that they made a mistake would be a major ego downer, resulting in making them *feel very bad about themselves*. Moreover, *in their subjective reality,* the mistake would be seen by the whole world as a major failure. In an attempt to avoid that feeling, these individuals will find themselves under the control of their Beast; a Beast anxious to stay in denial, denial, denial! Often they will remain in denial even after their ship has sunk and their job lost, continuing to find other reasons than themselves for their company's failure.

How can this situation be corrected?

We know a few things. First, the Beast wants to feel good about itself. Second, we know that most CEO's are highly intelligent, respect intelligence in others, and are anxious to continue to be perceived as highly intelligent. Third, we know that CEO's like all intelligent people, are well aware of the power of egos to misguide people. Finally, we also know that the ability to control oneself is extremely difficult. The Talmud and other Eastern and Western philosophies and religions also extol the virtue of self-control by the individual as one of the greatest attributes to be achieved in life. Therefore, the way to persuade the CEO to see the truth is to have him understand that it is his Beast/limbic brain seeking to feel good about itself that is denying the truth. This realization, alone, constitutes a manifestation of a very high level of intelligence and self-knowledge that in and of itself can and often will provide the limbic brain with the feeling good about itself satisfaction that it previously received from denying the truth. That could and should often result in the CEO recognizing and hopefully embracing his ability to see and correct his own errors as an indication of his superior intelligence and ability to control his own Beast.

Chapter Sixteen

State Interests

All human interaction can be seen as relationships of one kind or another. All relationships should benefit by a greater understanding of what causes them to be good or bad. Therefore, all relationships could and should profit from the application of these theories. Until now, we have considered the application of the principles in this book to one-on-one relationships, by individuals seeking to improve their own happiness and sense of feeling good about themselves and helping others achieve the same goal.

We now turn our attention to the state's interest in good relationships. Beyond the problems of suicide bombers, there are at least two other major areas in which the state has what is known in law as a compelling interest. Those areas are schools and general law enforcement.

In the USA the State has an obligation to provide schooling for all its citizens from at least first grade to grade twelve. It also has an obligation to protect its citizens by providing law and order at all times.

In executing its mandate, the state has to cope with several major problems. In some schools the state has to improve the current level of education and control or eliminate bullying and school gangs. In law enforcement, the state has to control street gangs everywhere and prison gangs in correctional facilities and/or prisons and jails.

Education: Improving learning

There is strong anecdotal evidence to suggest that making students 'feel good about themselves' by raising their self esteem can be a critical factor in helping them learn. Two movies based on real life experiences support that idea.

'Stand and Deliver' and 'Lean on Me'

The first is called *Stand and Deliver (1988).* In that film a dedicated teacher called Jaime Escalante, played by Edward James Olmos, inspires his dropout prone students to learn calculus so well that they are accused of cheating. He believed that students will rise to the level of expectation. His students did not believe they could learn calculus until he persuaded them that indeed they could. It is apparently that belief and the feeling good about themselves that arose from that belief that allowed them to become successful.

The second movie is a Warner Bros production called *Lean on Me* starring Morgan Freeman as the principal of Eastside High School in Patterson, New Jersey. The film tells the story of the takeover of a completely dysfunctional school by a dedicated and very strong willed principal called Joe Clark. Like Escalante, Clark believed in reinforcing 'pride in self and school' on a daily basis. He told his students that they could and would make it and it was clear that he believed it.

By saying and doing what he did he made the students believe what he believed, and that made them feel good about themselves by increasing their self esteem. That was apparently one critical key to their success. The other was discipline.

Teaching with Love

In his book called *Intelligence and How to Get it. (2009),* Richard E Nisbitt looks at the same problem. In Chapter Four, *Improving the Schools,* he addresses the importance of individual teachers in the lives of their students and what it is that makes them effective.

He speaks anecdotally of one exceptional teacher, whom he calls Miss A, whose students all remembered her name when they were adults and who otherwise gave her top grades. Miss A expressed confidence that all her students could learn. They said she 'taught with love'. They said she would stay late and tutor them on her own time, and even sometimes share her lunch with a student who had forgotten hers. As a result, outcomes in elementary school, in youth, and in adult life were much better for Miss A's students.

Teaching with 'love' is one way of 'showing love' which is a key factor in making another person 'feel good about herself'. Making another person feel good about herself seems to be a key factor in the learning process.

Nesbitt also provides convincing, quantitative evidence of what he calls the 'importance of teachers' in the learning process. His evidence comes from education researchers Bridget Hamre and Robert Pianta and their access to the National Institute of Child Health and Human Development sponsored 'huge longitudinal Study of Early Child Care'.

One conclusion reached by Hamre and Pianta was that the level of 'emotional support' received by the students could significantly improve learning in at least some of the students. Nesbitt notes that *'on the other hand there is little evidence to suggest that certification and higher degrees are associated with better teaching, and beyond the first year or so of teaching, neither is seniority.'* And what is 'emotional support' if not the desire, ability and practice of making students feel good about themselves?

In fact it would seem reasonable to suggest that if neither certification, higher degrees, nor seniority beyond one year, are associated with better teaching, shouldn't all teachers make a point of concentrating on the one thing that seems to work – to wit giving the students 'emotional support' by making them feel good about themselves?

Providing a level of emotional support sufficient to make a material difference to a child's education is not always as easy as it may sound. Helping teachers understand and assist students to learn through the provision of adequate emotional support is one of the things this book is about.

Education - School Bullying

Bullying is defined by Wikipedia, the free encyclopedia, www.en.wikipedia.org as *"an act of repeated aggressive behavior in order to intentionally hurt another person, physically or mentally"*

A bully is a person who is habitually cruel or overbearing especially to smaller or weaker people. These definitions do not adequately describe the kind of hell that students who are bullied sometimes have to endure. Bullies have been known to continually harass weaker students, hurt them, steal their books and money, humiliate them in ways that are unmentionable, and perhaps even sexually abuse them.

Moreover, bullying is not always limited to school grounds. Bullies may deliberately stalk their victims off campus to avoid potential intervention by school authorities.

We live in a violent society. The second amendment to the Constitution allows our people to carry guns. Guns are not hard to find if someone wants them badly enough. Knives have always been available. Thus, the threat of actually being killed, wounded, or maimed constitutes a real threat to victims in certain cases.

That sometimes forces victims to suffer the evils they know rather than risk greater evils by complaining. In turn, relief from bullies is difficult to obtain. Bullies are usually physically stronger than their victims. Complaints about bullying may bring worse punishment as retribution. Witnesses are fearful of talking lest they too become victims.

The school authorities and the police are hamstrung by laws and the US Constitution in ways that are well-intended, but that nevertheless makes it very difficult to fully protect victims from bullies. The ultimate rebellion against bullying by some students who can't take it any more is to shoot up the school, sometimes taking innocent lives, some of whom may themselves have been victims of bullies.

The result is that many options are being explored to prevent bullying, but all available evidence suggests that the results are far from satisfactory.

How to make others do something.

One can only make another do as one wants by *making the other person want to do it.* There are only two ways to do this, by *force or persuasion.* Force is punishment, and/or the fear of punishment. Persuasion makes the other person *want* to comply, and *not because he is afraid not to.*

People resent being punished. It makes them want to continue the forbidden behavior, though they will likely be more careful so as to avoid further punishment. Persuasion creates a more lasting change. That is a good thing for both the persuader and the one persuaded, and in this case, the victim.

Let's now examine the mindset of the bully in the context of our theories. *(The approach suggested may or may not work in particular instances, but it should be a significant improvement over existing policies.)*

A bully, like everybody else, possesses two separate 'personalities' the Beast and the Logical Me. Anecdotal evidence about bullies indicates that they did not have happy childhoods. That means that they did not receive the kind of 'emotional capital' necessary to keep their Beast in check. So what tends to happen is that their 'Beast' substitutes a '*bad source feel good'* sense for the unavailable *feeling good about itself.*

That *bad source feel good* sense comes from the exercise of abusive power over weaker victims, commonly known as bullying. Unless and until that *bad source feel good* substitute is replaced with a sense of *feeling good about itself,* only coercive power of 'force' can be used to try to stop bullying.

Coercive power is a deterrent. It is the power to punish *after the fact* with the hope that the punishment will stop further bullying. It works through the fear of being punished. Regrettably, most often all it does is make the bully more careful about not being caught.

It is not likely to make the bully want to stop bullying. The suggestion is that providing the feeling good about itself craved by the bully's Beast, will eliminate the need for bullying.

The question now becomes–*Can this be done, and if so, how?* Yes it can be done. Not in all cases however. The following approaches should work at least some of the time. If they work at all, these methods may well provide a permanent answer to the problem. Moreover, applying these methods is quick and relatively easy. Little will be lost if they fail.

The technique discussed in the section on *Business Interests* applies here. It is the idea that *merely becoming aware of one's own Beast ability to take over one's Logical Me* and produce bad behavior of one sort or another will provide the *feeling good about oneself* craved by the Beast.

This happens because the Beast recognizes its own major insight and that shows considerable intelligence. Recognizing such a high level of intelligence should be enough to make the Beast *feel good about itself* and remove the need to bully others just to *feel good.*

However, this technique may or may not work for those whose intelligence fails to see the connection, or whose Beast's power is particularly strong.

If the first effort fails, then the second part of the system should be attempted. This part involves providing the bully with a socially acceptable alternative that will give the bully his feeling good about himself as an acceptable substitute to his Beast/limbic brain for his anti-social behavior.

For example, a bully could be made the protector of particular victims of either himself or other bullies. Providing the bully with *a responsibility to protect* might work as a substitute to the alternative of bullying. Particularly since it would be a role in which the bully would be able to exercise power, but for good, not evil. Other supervised responsibilities might be given a bully to show that the school believes he can change. It is what Dale Carnegie talked about in his perennial best seller, *How to Win Friends and Influence People,* when he suggested that one *"give a bad dog a good name."*

Bullying: the Boynton Beach experience

In 1979 I was building a number of homes in the City of Boynton Beach, Florida. The homes were on lots scattered throughout an existing development where many people were already living. There came a time when the houses under construction were being vandalized. I would show up every morning and find that someone had been in some of the houses and deliberately broken pipes, windows and made holes in the drywall.

I called the police who came and investigated. Their conclusion was that the vandalism was being perpetrated by a very small group of 10 -13 year old school kids. But they also added that unless the kids were caught red handed they could do nothing about it. Catching the kids red handed would only be possible if I hired a night watchman to keep an eye on all the houses every night and weekends. Of course if I did have a night watchman the kids would know it and avoid vandalizing, and would never get caught. The problem was that the cost of a night watchman for 5 nights a week and all weekend was prohibitive.

I knew the neighborhood and I knew the names of the kids who were vandalizing the homes. There were only 5 kids in the immediate neighborhood. I had spoken to all of them and of course they had denied any knowledge of the vandalism. They did have a leader. So I decided to speak to him.

With his parent's approval I offered him a few dollars a week if he would agree to "supervise" my property and make sure there was no vandalism. His payment would be contingent on the total absence of vandalism. I thus made him "supervisor" of my project in the off hours. I gave the "bad dog" a good name as well as a few dollars in "encouragement" to remain vigilant. The vandalism stopped immediately.

I realized that all his responsibilities as "supervisor" required was his decision to tell his "gang" as their leader that they were to stop vandalizing my property. However, he did seem to feel very *good about himself* that I trusted him to supervise my property, and of course the few dollars helped.

Law Enforcement - school, street and prison gangs

A "gang" is defined by Wikipedia –www.en.wikipedia.org–as "*a group of people who, through the organization, formation, and establishment of an assemblage, share a common identity.*" In layman's terms, it means a criminal organization or else a group with a criminal affiliation. According to Wikipedia– www.en.wikipedia.org – there were at least 30,000 gangs and 800,000 gang members active in the USA in 2007.

Gangs often establish special ways to identify themselves. These ways include tattoos, tags, particular colors, signs, flags, secret greetings, slurs or code words, or other special symbols to define and differentiate themselves from other gangs. Gang members generally come from dysfunctional homes and have often been mentally, physically, or sexually abused or some combination of all three.

They grow up with low self-esteem, virtually no emotional capital, and very little sense of *'belonging'* to either their biological families or the society in which they live. As a result of these problems, they tend to do poorly in school and drop out early. All of these factors tend to provide them with very few marketable skills and an inability to do more than barely make a living.

Moreover, as individuals all too often just trying to survive in the streets in bad neighborhoods that victimize them, they often find themselves in desperate need of some kind of alliances in order to quite literally stay alive. This is where the idea of joining a gang may enter their minds. They see gang members enjoying a sense of family and protection from the dangers of the streets.

From their perception and *subjective reality* they are completely right. Most often, there are also financial benefits from a gang's criminal activities; activities viewed as impossible for a non-gang member to achieve alone. They see non-gang members like themselves become victims of gangs, even when they are trying to live minimal existences within the law.

Therefore, faced with nothing but bad life choices, they often choose what they see as the lesser of two evils, and they join a gang. The price they generally have to pay is a pledge of absolute loyalty, obedience to the leader, and a willingness to participate in criminal activities. The benefits they get are protection, affection, a sense of belonging to a family, and some of the spoils of criminal activity.

Sometimes they are even required to pay the price of admission to the gang. That price can range, for females, to submitting to sexual activity with all male gang members, or for males, to submitting to gang beatings, or specific criminal acts like stealing, beating up a member of a rival gang, or occasionally murdering someone.

Gangs exist in force in prisons and in our streets, and to a lesser degree, in our schools. They constitute an evil force that corrupts youth and is very active in all major criminal activities. Gangs are often viewed as having far too much control of the nation's prisons, and are the source of high-dollar costs, crimes, and ruined lives throughout the nation.

The battle against gangs has been going on since at least 1850, at which time, Wikipedia – www.en.wikipedia.org – reports, as many as 200 gang wars were fought in New York City alone.

Gangs exist as forms of independent cultures within the greater society in which they function. They make their own rules of behavior, set the 'price of admission' to the gang, and penalties for failing to comply with their rules. Penalties are harsh and usually involve very serious consequences including severe beatings, fines, and even death. Leaving a gang is rarely an option. Attempts to leave may well give rise to the execution of the person attempting to leave.

Gangs and their members constitute the hardest of all situations to correct. Individuals need to be taught to overcome their own Beast in order to go from negative to positive behavior.

In a marital or other one-on-one situation, one individual is trying to help another to change bad behavior into good. Ordinarily, both persons' values will mirror the value of the society in which they live. Therefore, changing from negative to positive behavior will require the person changing from behavior society is against to behavior which society approves. For example, a spouse trying to get another to stop verbal or physical abuse, alcoholism, or drug use etc. will be acting in way society approves.

However, when the greater society through the courts, schools, or prison systems, tries to correct antisocial behavior by gang members loyal to their own particular set of values, the task is much harder.

For example, it is viewed as a good thing for law abiding citizens to report crimes and as much information as possible for identifying the criminals to the authorities. However, gang members generally regard informing on other members as "ratting" them out and therefore a very bad thing. Within the gang culture or gang societal rules that is viewed as an act of betrayal, cowardice, and disloyalty, often punishable by death.

The Informer

A 1935 dramatic film titled *The Informer* illustrates this point very well. The film is set in 1922 and concerns the Irish War of Independence. Ireland was under British rule and many Irish citizens wanted independence from Britain. The main 'society rules' were British law. The outlaws, or those that can be viewed as similar in cultural outlook as outlaw gangs, were dedicated to the independence of Ireland, which at the time was considered treasonous behavior under the law.

In the film, a brutish, but well-meaning Irishman, Gypo Nolan, informs on his best friend, a member of the Irish Republican Army, for a twenty pound reward. The film traces his conscience ridden emotional disintegration that eventually leads him to give himself away.

The conflict here is between personal interest and loyalty to a friend and a cause in which he believed. Though different in specifics, it is very similar to what a gang member faces when pressed to name his criminal accomplices. Should he take the reward the authorities offer in the form of some kind of reduced sentence in exchange for betraying his friends and family? Or should he stand firm and suffer the consequences of loyalty?

It is important when attempting to persuade a gang member of some point of view that authorities recognize the gang member's values are very different for the general society in which he lives, and therefore adjust their approach accordingly.

Chapter Seventeen

Religion

The Judeo-Christian-Muslim religions all recognize the same origins and the Ten Commandment as God's law given to Moses on Mount Sinai. The Catholic religion has identified seven sins it regards as 'cardinal sins' to which it asserts man is subject.

It would be interesting to analyze God's law and the Catholic seven deadly sins in terms of the Beast within us.

The Ten Commandments are a list of do's and don'ts and start with the 'don'ts'.

Eight instructions order us *not to*: have other gods; make graven images; take the name of the Lord in vain; kill; commit adultery; steal; bear false witness or covet.

Two instructions order us to: Remember the Sabbath and honor thy father and mother.

The Seven Deadly sins are also known as Capital Vices or Cardinal Sins[44] These sins are listed as:

1.Lust.2.Gluttony, 3. Greed/Avarice; 4. Sloth/
Laziness; 5.Wrath/Anger; 6.Envy; 7. Pride/Hubris.

It is interesting to note that our Beast, in an attempt to "feel good" when it very much wants to 'feel good about itself' but cannot, turns to many if not most, of the

[44] Wikepedia, the free encyclopedia

seven deadly sins and disobedience of many of God's commandments. For example the Beast turns to:

1. ***Lust:*** which is excessive sexual activity and "coveting" and perhaps actively engaging in sexual activity with the coveted person.
2. ***Gluttony:*** which is overeating or over drinking or overindulgence of anything to the point of waste.
3. ***Greed/Avarice:*** Described as a very excessive or rapacious desire and pursuit of wealth, status and power.
4. ***Sloth/Laziness:*** Described as laziness and indifference
5. ***Wrath/Anger:*** Also called 'rage' is described as inordinate and uncontrolled feelings of hatred and anger.
6. ***Envy:*** Described by Dante Alighieri as " love of one's own good perverted to desire to deprive other men of theirs"
7. ***(Excessive) Pride:*** Also known as Hubris, is a desire to be more important or attractive than others, failing to acknowledge the good work of others and excessive love of self. Dante's definition is "love of self perverted to hatred and contempt for one's neighbor".

Without going into too much detail, it is very clear that the Beast within us when seeking to "feel good" often turns to disobeying God's laws by killing, committing adultery; stealing; bearing false witness or coveting and sexually engaging others inappropriately. Similarly, the Beast will turn to being guilty of one or more of the Seven Deadly Sins by lustful sexual activity (lust); excessive eating and drinking and consuming drugs (gluttony); pursuing wealth and power rapaciously and without regard for the rights of others (greed); refuse to do meaningful productive work (sloth); abuse others verbally and physically (wrath/anger); Be envious of others (envy); fail to acknowledge the good work of others and believe in his own omnipotence.

It could be of interest to theologians to trace human behavior resulting in breaking God's laws and/or indulging in the seven cardinal sins, to the possibility of the absence of emotional currency and emotional capital accumulation in the early years.

Chapter Eighteen

Sociology

Sociology is defined as: *The study of society, human social interaction, and the rules and processes that bind and separate people not only as individuals, but as members of associations, groups, and institutions.*[45] Sociology deals with the creation of groupings in society and what makes them cohesive. Basic human motivations are very much in play here too.

Ethnocentrism is the tendency to believe that one's own race or ethnic group is the most important and that some or all aspects of its culture are superior to those of other groups.[46]

Prejudice is defined as any preconceived opinion or feeling, whether positive or negative[47].

It is a given that survival is the highest human motivation. To survive, man first banded into family groups and then tribal groups. Eventually the tribes created settlements that grew into towns and then united into countries. The original purpose of 'banding together' was to increase the chances of the group over the individual or smaller group, to acquire

[45] See en.wiktionary.org/wiki/sociology

[46] See en.wikipedia.org/wiki/Ethnocentrism

[47] See en.wiktionary.org/wiki/prejudice

the necessities for survival, to wit: food, water, shelter and security.

But other groups were also ‘banding together’ for the same purposes. Moreover the things necessary for survival and later for those things beyond survival, were in limited supply. Other groups also wanted them.

To strengthen one’s own group and weaken others the concept of ethnocentrism was born. Each group told its members that *their group* was superior to all others. That kept the group together and minimized the desire of members to look for other ‘better groups’.

Telling one’s group that its members are ‘better’ in some important way unavoidably also tells members that all others are ‘worse’ in some way. You cannot be ‘better’ than someone unless that someone is ‘worse’ than you!

Believing that someone is ‘worse’ than you when you have no other knowledge of that someone is called a ‘preconceived opinion’ and is also one dictionary definition of ‘prejudice’.

So our Beast is trained to think he is ‘better’ than certain others. Often it is a short step from there to ‘dislike’ the others he thinks lesser than himself. From there to ‘hating’ them, particularly if they are somehow doing ‘better’ than he is, may not take long.

Current societal economic groupings:

The ‘ethnocentric’ group battle for economic advancement continues within every civilized society. Within our own society we have the following ‘groupings’ of individuals all seeking their own best economic interests over that of all others: Unions, professional associations, political parties, business associations, ethnic associations, religious associations, etc.,

To be sure all of these groups usually profess to be seeking the public good in one form or another. That helps their legitimacy and helps to play down their selfish intentions. Often, many members of these groups sincerely believe the altruistic pronouncements of their leaders. But there can be no doubt that the economic advancement of their members is one of their most significant goals. Group leaders who do not understand that will rarely survive long as leaders.

PART IV

Chapter Nineteen

Why I wrote this book

As a practical man I have no desire to write about what is already known. Moreover statistics indicate that the majority of books by unknown authors (like me) have to be "self published" at the author's expense, and are very likely to lose money. So I didn't do it for the money. Why then did I write this book?

It was done as a labor of love. I am a self styled philosopher who is a lover of wisdom and therefore a seeker of knowledge and truth. It was truth about relationships (or at least a significant part of truth), which I sought and believed I found, that led me to write this book.

The beginning of the search

Ever since I read *How to Win Friends and Influence People* I became aware of the need to "make people feel important" when dealing with them. However what I could not find in any book was how to resolve my next problems, which were:

> *Why was I constantly and uncontrollably thinking derogatory thoughts about others?*

> *Why couldn't I easily and constantly apply the Dale Carnegie philosophy?*
> *Why was I unable to control my bad habit of often being aggressively disagreeable towards others?*
> *Was there anything I could do to understand the cause and therefore hopefully to learn how to control that undesirable behavior?*

My questions addressed the fundamental processes and mysteries of human behavior. That is the area of expertise of Psychology. So I decided to read as much as I could about that subject. Over a period of years and with the help of my friend and mentor Dr. Hoffman, I learned all I could about the field of human behavior as currently explained by psychology.

The first question for which I sought an answer was: *Is Psychology a Science? If not a science, what exactly is it?*

The details of what I learned about Science and Psychology can be found in **Appendix I** of this book. Basically I discovered that:

- Psychology is not yet a science
- Nobody has articulated any general theory of human behavior that is verifiable or that can predict human behavior accurately.

My next step was to proceed with my own research and attempt to reach my own conclusions.

My research and conclusions

Operating through self analysis and introspection and as much informal experimentation and verification as I could accomplish, I came to the following conclusions:

The first, which I call the Ronald Bibace Theory of Personality states: *All human behavior past survival seeks to make individuals feel good about themselves and avoid feeling bad about themselves.*

That Theory of Personality may also be referred to as the Ronald Bibace Universal Theory of Human Behavior. That is because it encompasses in a single clear statement the motivation that seems to drive all human activity.

The process began when I discovered what all available evidence indicates is the key ingredient in all good human relationships, *which is the need we each have to feel good about ourselves.*

I then tested the results anecdotally by means of the Self Test described earlier in this book. The statistical results, though unscientific, were overwhelming positive. Encouraged by the result I continued my research to determine how one could achieve the desired goal, what the obstacles to the goal were and how to overcome those obstacles. The further conclusions were:

- *The desire to feel good about ourselves is "one side of a single coin", the other side is the desire to avoid feeling bad about oneself.*
- *We each possess within our brain an "illogical limbic Beast" often in conflict with our Logical brain.*
- *The Beast within us can be very powerful and make us act in ways we disapprove of without us even being aware of what is happening.*
- *We can learn to control that Beast by means of the Magic switch.*

I continued further introspection and anecdotal testing and application of these ideas. The methodology of my research can be found in Appendix II.

The results once more persuaded me that my overall approach appeared valid and led to the writing of this book. For further confirmation that my theories were sufficiently different from conventional wisdom, I listed the differences between the theories in this book and conventional wisdom in the field. That list can be found in Appendix III.

What about predicting behavior?

The essence of any scientific theory is that it can predict behavior. Prediction is defined as: *the act of foretelling; also, that which is foretold.* [1913 Webster]. I believe that the application of the Ronald Bibace Universal Theory of Human behavior can predict behavior. Some may regard what are referred to here as 'predictions' are merely 'theories'. In any case they do seem to constitute a step forward in knowledge about human behavior.

Predictions or theories?

The following are a number of 'predictions' that I suggest can be made based on my theory. Here they are:

1. *Testing bullies, gang members and criminals for the low level of emotional currency received in their youth and thus the potential lack of emotional capital accumulated, will result in a statistically significant lower level of emotional capital for those groups than for the general population.*

2. *Testing "false profile" criminals for the same emotional capital levels will produce the same results as testing "high or true profile" criminals. A false profile criminal is one whose comfortable or even opulent lifestyle and upbringing may falsely suggest that the criminal falls outside the expected*

profile of the "boy from the hood" beaten by a drunken father and a crack addict mother.

3. *Testing couples who get along well, for their levels of emotional capital, will result in numbers sufficiently different from the "norm" or average of all couples as to be statistically significant. Couples who get along well will be much more likely to have accumulated sufficient emotional capital to sustain them in times of stress.*

4. *Testing couples who have continual difficulty getting along should result in lower numbers of emotional capital sufficiently different from the "norm" of all couples as to be statistically significant.*

5. *Applying society approved methods that make anti-social individuals feel good about themselves will result in a statistically significant reduction of anti-social behavior.*

On the quality and effectiveness of advice:

In order for change to occur in a person's behavior it is essential that the person learn what to do, how to do it, how to recognize obstacles to the desired behavior and finally how to overcome those obstacles. The learning process may occur from personal insight. Most often however, it will occur through listening to advice from others.

That brings us to the question of *what kind of advice*. For advice to trigger change it must both be good, which refers to its quality, and effective, which refers to how well it achieves its goals.

What is good advice?

How do we define 'good advice'? One definition would be: *advice which, if followed, will achieve the desired goal.* For example if a person wants to lose weight, probably the best advice ever given is: *Eat less and exercise more.* Or if a person wants to be able to retire in some comfort, then good advice would be: *Start saving regularly and when you are young, don't borrow money, and don't live beyond your means.*

Is the advice effective?

Often this kind of excellent advice is already known to those with the related problems. So the next question is: *Is the advice effective?* For advice to be *effective*, it should be enable the listener to follow it and achieve her goals.

The world abounds with advice on good relationships. Almost one million psychologists and psychiatrists in the US alone, make it at least part of their business to help their patients improve their relationships. Clergymen regard it as an important part of their duties to help members of their congregations and faith get along better together and with all others. There are also an overwhelming number of books, magazines, TV programs, and online relationship advice specialists ready to help those in need.

Beginning with the admonition to "do unto others as you would have them do unto you" there is a proliferation of good advice from professionals whose job is primarily, or at least partially, involved with the giving of advice to improve relationships. The advice these professionals give may differ in emphasis somewhat from one group to another, but in general there is at least a broad consensus on many things people could do to improve their relationships. The section in this book on what many professionals agree as to which behavior to adopt and which to avoid, describes that very broad consensus.

Clearly there is an abundant availability of 'good quality' advice. The question is: *How effective is it?*

What makes advice effective?

What kind of advice is likely to achieve the desired goals? For starters let us recognize that there are two kinds of advice; *the general and the specific.*

General advice: General advice is nice but not very helpful. That is because it usually only defines a goal, but not how to achieve it. One example is: *Do unto others as you would have them do unto you.* Another is: *To live long, stay healthy.* Neither admonition tells how to achieve the stated goal, and is therefore only marginally helpful.

Let us call this level of good advice – Level One – worth no more than a 1 on a 1-10 scale, because it is only general advice

Specific advice: Specific advice is better than general advice. It can also vary between somewhat specific and very specific. For example one could add to the general advice *do unto others...,* the following more specific advice: *Be nice, kind, considerate and forgiving to others.* Or, one could add to the general advice: *To live long, stay healthy...* the following more specific advice: *Keep your weight down, exercise regularly and avoid excesses of food and drink.* That advice is more specific and therefore more helpful

Let us call this level of good advice –Level Two-worth perhaps a 2 to 3 on a 1 to 10 scale, because it is more specific. The rating between a 2 and a 3 would depend on the level of specificity: the higher the specificity, the higher the rating.

Implementing good advice depends on knowledge of how to implement and simplicity of implementation.

Effective advice is also very much dependent on explaining how to implement good advice: Even very specific advice requires knowledge about implementation to be effective. It is often not enough to tell somebody to: *Be nice, kind, considerate and forgiving to others,* without also explaining in some detail how to do it.

For example one could say: *Always be polite to others, do small and big favors for them whenever possible, overcome your anger when they hurt you and smile and forgive them.*

Or one could add to the advice on staying healthy to live long: *Establish what the right weight is for your height and age; establish how many calories a day and how much exercise is needed to keep your weight at the desired level and stay within these parameters.*

Implementation is also dependent on the simplicity of the advice. The simpler the advice the easier it is to remember and therefore to implement.

For example if one is told that in order to maintain good relationships one should remember 12 do's and 4 don'ts, or a total of 16 separate recommended positive and negative behaviors, one is not very likely to be able to remember and implement them. Whereas if one is asked to remember one simple rule: *Make the other person feel good about herself,* one is far more likely to remember and implement said rule

Let us call this level of good advice Level Three – worth perhaps a 4 to 5 on a 1 to 10 scale, because it includes information on how to implement it. The rating between a 4 and 5 would depend on the level of simplicity; the simpler the advice the higher the score.

Effective advice must also recognize the existence of any obvious as well as any concealed obstacles that may exist in virtually all of us that may be blocking our ability to follow the advice received.

All too often people have received very good and very specific advice (say at a 5 on our 1-10 scale) and have also been taught how to implement the advice – but they still can't do it! That is because there are obstacles blocking the implementation of the advice. That is when it becomes imperative to identify the obstacles, both obvious and concealed, and to do so as specifically as possible. All too often the major obstacle to correcting behavior is concealed. Without identifying the concealed obstacle, it is usually either very difficult or impossible to overcome. That is because one can hardly overcome something one is not even aware exists!

For example: A wife in a difficult marital relationship who may be told to *always be polite to her husband, do small and big favors for him and overcome her anger when he upsets her,* will often respond that she simply can't do it. She cannot overcome her anger, period!

The obvious obstacle is the anger. She knows that. But what of any concealed obstacles?

Until she recognizes and learns to cope with the 'concealed obstacle' her chances of correcting her behavior are very poor. Moreover the concealed obstacle may well be not merely blocking overcoming the obstacle but also the *principal trigger* to the visible anger reaction.

But what if she learns and understands that her concealed obstacle is the Beast within her that takes control of her logical mind and secretly does with her as it wishes! That is useful information.

Let us call this Level Four – worth perhaps a 6 on the 1-10 scale of advice effectiveness.

Effective advice must also provide a method for overcoming the obstacles indentified.

If one is told one has incurable cancer, one can better prepare for death, but the information is not otherwise very helpful. But if one is diagnosed with cancer that is curable in time to cure it, and also told how to cure it, then one has truly achieved something worthwhile. So it is with discovering all the obstacles to one's desired behavior. If one can both discover what the obstacles are and also learn the secret of how to overcome them, one has achieved knowledge about how to achieve the pinnacle of behavior modification.

Let us call this Level Five – worth perhaps a 7 to 8 on the 1-10 scale.

Successful implementation of the learned procedure for overcoming obstacles will provide the highest level of success.

If one is successfully trained to identify the Beast as the hidden obstacle and then trained to overcome the beast with the "Magic Switch" described in this book, then behavior will have been successfully modified.

<u>We will call this ultimate level, Level Six – worth anywhere from a 9 to a 10, depending on how completely and permanently the behavior modification has occurred.</u>

Why this theory now?

The theory has not been scientifically tested. So why not wait? The reason for writing about it now is two-fold. The first is that proving any *theory of personality* scientifically may well be impossible, at least within the foreseeable future. The second is that obtaining formal approval by established authorities can take ten to twenty years. That is true even for experts in the field, let alone for one who like myself, lacks 'acknowledged credentials'.

The difficulty faced by all new ideas

New ideas are hard-pressed to gain acceptance, even among professionals. *A General Theory of Love* (printed in January 2001 by Vintage Press, New York) is a book on the science of human emotions by Thomas Lewis M.D., an assistant clinical professor of psychiatry at the University of California, Fari Amini, M.D a professor of Psychiatry at the UCSF School of Medicine, and Richard Lannon, M.D., an associate clinical professor of psychiatry at the UCSF School of Medicine.

Page 143 of that book contains the following statement: "*Because human beings remember with neurons, we are disposed to see more of what we have already seen, hear anew what we have heard most often, think just we have always thought. .... A wistful aside from two neuroscience researchers: [In] scientific work we find that new theories are understood only by graduate students, whose intellectual identities are then wholly transformed**...In contrast, the***

senior professors are burdened with such conventional inertia that when they encounter new ideas there is no apparent effect, other than an occasional vague irritation." (Emphasis added)

It is true that the vast majority of new ideas are unworthy. That may well be why experts in particular fields tend to be very skeptical.

However, what is also true is that all human progress is entirely dependent on the very small number of new ideas that are worthy.

What seems indisputable, even among professionals, is that their efforts to improve relationships produce results that are often less than satisfying in spite of the great deal of effort and personal commitment by the individuals involved.

The apparent flaws in existing theories

The reason that existing theories appear flawed is because there are so many. Moreover, because all the evidence appears to support the conclusion that few if any recognize the basic forces that control interpersonal behavior. That explains why only occasional and often less than satisfactory results are obtained by existing methods.

Sundry Comments

On the originality of the ideas

Some people have argued that the idea that making others feel good about themselves is not new and therefore hardly worthy of a book. While it is true that everybody recognizes that self-esteem is important to us all, and that a high level of self-esteem and feeling good about oneself are very closely related, ***nobody has ever identified the concept of feeling***

good about oneself as the key critical ingredient in all human relationships.

This identification as the key ingredient is critically important. Because it is only after that occurs that one can begin to examine the next set of questions. To wit: 1) how does one achieve that? 2) What obstacles must be overcome to achieving that? And finally 3) how does one overcome those obstacles?

Scientific progress can only be made one step at a time. Thus, for as long as the belief prevails that there are many possible answers to the question of good relationships, only limited progress is possible.

It is not unlike being told that a pot of gold lies at the end of a maze, the entrance to which has a dozen doors. *But only a single door can eventually lead to the pot of gold.* Therefore, one must first identify the right door to the maze before one can even hope to begin the search that will eventually reach the pot of gold. In this case, the doors are not even very clearly marked and none at all are marked *feeling good about oneself.*

On the value of existing methods and their relationship to the theories in this book

What about the existing guidelines as listed in the do's and don'ts subscribed to by so many professionals? Do they work? If they do, how does that relate to this new theory?

The first problem with the do's and don'ts is that there are too many of them. One top person in the field identifies as many as sixteen in all (Twelve do's and four don'ts). Remembering sixteen points at all times is a significant burden, even for a PhD. Even then, there is at least one example in which even if all of the "right" attitudes are present in both parties, the relationship is doomed.

The "perfect" US Marine Colonel and his "perfect" Marine Sergeant son.

Let's assume a "perfect" United States Marine Colonel has a United States Marine Sergeant son who is also "perfect" in every way, and by every societal standard. They respect each other, love each other, treat each other well, and do all things recommended by the experts in the field. Will that guarantee a good relationship?

Not if the father is a devout Catholic who believes the biblical admonition that homosexuality is an abomination and a mortal sin, and the son happens to be a homosexual!

In that situation, neither person can make the other feel good about himself. The father feels badly for having a gay son, and the son is made to feel badly by a father who rejects what he believes is a choice of lifestyle, and necessarily, the son who lives it. Therefore, their relationship can never be deemed good.

The problem with internalizing current wisdom

When making a mindset change, internalizing is essential. It is the process by which we eventually learn to do subconsciously that which we are training ourselves to do consciously. *It is a hard enough process when we are working with a single concept.* That is because our conscious minds can only think of a single thing at a time. Therefore, to act on, absorb, and internalize as many as twenty or more different concepts, *all more or less simultaneously*, is a monumental task, at which very few can hope to succeed.

The ounce of gold in the ton of ore

Yet, we know that some level of progress, for some people, does exist by the use of these methods. How does that happen? The answer is simple. *To the extent that any progress is made, all the evidence suggests that it is because within the mass of do's and don'ts there often exists a part of the essential core of making a person feel good about himself.* That feeling can be viewed as the 'ounce of gold' in the 'ton of ore' that the action constitutes.

What is the actual meaningful result of showing affection, or being responsible, affectionate, loyal, etc., *but to make another person feel worthy of such actions and therefore make that person feel good about himself?*

What is the result of Dale Carnegie's prime recommendation to sincerely make the other person feel important, but seeking to make the other person feel good about himself?

What is the actual meaningful result of avoiding behavior like nagging, criticism, complaining and stonewalling, or ignoring another etc., *if not to avoid making the other person feel bad about himself?*

Thus, all the recommended positive actions or negative action to be avoided are 'designed' to achieve the same fundamental results: *To make the person feel good about himself, or avoid making the person feel bad about himself.* It is that result which constitutes the "ounce of gold" in the "ton of ore".

Why then do current practices not work very often if they contain the ounce of gold? Because it seems to be extremely difficult to simultaneously remember all the recommended behaviors and because the failure to remember even one recommended action or inaction can undermine an entire relationship.

For example, a man can treat his wife with all the love, affection and kindness etc. that is required by her. But if he criticizes her, even occasionally for being too fat or a bad cook or a bad mother, or constantly complains about her in other ways, he will still fail to have a good relationship.

Many a wife given every golden material advantage has lived a very unhappy life with a husband who could not make her feel good about herself. Also, because only by making the other person feel good about herself can all the positives be included, and the negatives excluded, *simultaneously*

Finally because there are major unaddressed obstacles to the implementation of appropriate behavior. It is only by understanding those obstacles that one can hope to overcome them. Those obstacles can best be recognized, understood, and hopefully dealt with, by the methods explained in this book.

Specific issues addressed

The following are some of the specific issues I addressed in anticipation of possible concerns.

> *My results are not scientific:* That is true. However, where uncertainty is the norm is not *significantly less uncertainty* a sign of progress? Moreover in a field apparently devoid of results that meet the highest scientific standards on the issue of general theories of personality and human behavior, shouldn't apparently reasonable conclusions receive consideration and a fair hearing
>
> *Correlation is not cause*: Psychologists are taught that the mere presence of two events occurring in sequence does not *necessarily* mean that one *caused* the other. The point being that making a person feel good about herself appears to co-exist with or be followed by an improvement in a relationship, *is not scientific proof that the first caused the second.*

Be that as it may, it is at least suggestive of cause, and certainly not proof of the opposite. Moreover, in the total absence of any scientific proof of what indeed does cause such an improvement, it is reasonable to proceed on the working premise that one does cause the other.

Also, the more often the working premise is confirmed, the better the probability that causality does exist. The actual results, albeit anecdotal, are an overwhelmingly significant statistical confirmation of the concept. Surely that should be enough to encourage a person to try it, particularly if that can be done easily and inexpensively and with no apparent downside.

Everybody knows that making another person feel good about him/herself is important in relationships. Be that as it may, it is one thing to have a general idea of a thing's importance, it is quite another to identify it as the critical, key ingredient to all good relationships. Because that is what makes it the starting point of the discovery process and all further research, as well as the reason for the discovery of the key obstacle, the reasons for its presence and the manner to overcome it. Even if it is regarded as merely a question of emphasis it is still emphasis critical to achieving the desired outcome.

As a non-professional, my book will have little or no credibility. Such an attack would constitute an Aristotelian false argument known as "ad hominem." That is an attack on *who the person is and not on what he says.*

It is certainly possible that some may be persuaded by that argument. It is more likely that most intelligent, fair minded people, including professional psychologists, will recognize the false argument for what it is.

We live in an era of instant communication through the Internet. Good ideas will surface and bad ones will die quickly. No professional will want to be seen as refusing to consider a good idea because of its source. After all what is important is what idea is worth holding, not who originally held the idea.

How do we know your ideas are any good: When Ross Perot, the billionaire Texas businessman, was running for President of the United States in 1992, he was often asked questions about the value of some ideas he put forth. He would often reply, "*Compared to what?"*

His point being that any idea should be compared against systems then in place, not against some utopian ideal that might never be achievable. So the answer is: *The proof that the ideas are good is the overwhelmingly strong evidence, albeit anecdotal and unscientific, supporting the fact that the ideas work and virtually none that suggest that the ideas do not. That is a result that compares very favorably with all existing systems, and therefore should be worthy of serious consideration.*

Conclusion

To the general public, I respectfully suggest that since the concept is relatively easy to understand, internalize, and apply, can show results very quickly, and has very little downside, it is well worth trying. Good luck!

To the professionals in the field who have been kind enough to read this book and who realize that these ideas 'challenge the norm' I respectfully suggest:

Do not seek what the ideas may fail to do, but rather seek what they offer that may constitute progress in human knowledge and in the understanding of human behavior.

APPENDIX I

Science And Psychology

Psychologists coined a phrase for 'general theories of human behavior' which they term 'Personality Theory' or 'Theory of Personality'. The McGraw-Hill Dictionary of Scientific and Technical Terms (6th Edition) defines "Personality Theory" as *'A branch of psychology concerned with developing a scientifically defensible model or view of human behavior'.*

That was exactly what I was looking for. So I sought out that *'scientifically defensible model of human behavior'* and I quickly discovered that ***none exists.***

What knowledge does exist? My main authority on the subject is a book called *Beneath the Mask*, *An Introduction to Theories of Personality*, 2003, Seventh Edition, by Christopher E. Monte and Robert N. Sollod. However, before examining the details of what exists, let us review the opinion of the authors on the general status of the field of psychology. In Chapter 19 of their book the authors' state:

So many of the theories presented in this book are neither testable nor have been adequately tested. This prompts us to ask two questions:

1. *Is there any reasonable way to decide which theory is right?*
2. *If psychology is a science, why does it tolerate so many unscientific theories?*

The answer seems to be that the *'science'* of psychology is still in its infancy, and clearly not yet quite a science. Science began with the early Greek Philosophers, known as pre-Socratics, speculating about the nature of the universe. Aristotle referred to them as 'Investigators of Nature". The first philosopher/scientists were thinkers. They expressed opinions and theories that were "intelligent speculation" and that were not testable at the time. Sometimes these "theories" were diametrically opposed to one another.

Thus Thales, reputed to be the father of Greek Philosophy, declared water to be the basis of all things. Anaximenes, another original 'Philosopher' thought all things came from fire, wind, earth and water. Democritus believed in the doctrine of atoms. He thought that all things were composed of indivisible small bodies uniting in different ways to become the objects of the universe. None of these "theories" were verifiable at the time. However, as a Chinese proverb says: *A thousand mile trip starts with a single step.* The first step on the trip to scientific knowledge started with these Greek Philosopher Investigators of Nature.

So the question arises: How close to being a science is psychology, if it does not present any testable theories? To find out I researched the following questions:

- *What exactly is the definition of science? And*
- *Based on that definition how scientific is the current knowledge in the field of Psychology*?

What is science?

According to Webster's New Collegiate Dictionary *science* is described as: *Knowledge covering general truths of the operation of general laws, esp. as obtained and tested through scientific method (and) concerned with the physical world.*

The scientific method is a process for experimentation that is used to explore observations and answer questions. It is a method to search for cause and effect relationships in nature. Briefly it involves:

Constructing a hypothesis; testing it by experimentation; analyzing the data and drawing conclusions and finally communicating the results.

It is important that the experiment be a fair test. A fair test occurs when you change only one factor (variable) and keep all other conditions the same.[48]

Unfortunately there exists no *general theory of human behavior* that is postulated by any psychologist. Moreover, whatever "resultant ideas" have been produced by psychologists involve far more than one variable. That means they cannot be subjected to the kind of "fair test" requirement of no more than a single variable. That re-affirms the idea that psychology is not quite yet a science[49].

My understanding of the status of Psychology today

The authors of Beneath the Mask, list 19 theorists in the field, broken down into 9 categories. The names of the theorists and the categories of the theories they subscribe to are:

[48] See www.sciencebuddies.org

[49] See www.sciencebuddies.org

- Classical Psychoanalysis: *Sigmund Freud* (Freud is the recognized founder of the discipline)
- Ego Psychology: *Erik Erikson, Anna Freud, and Margaret Mahler*
- Object Relations Theory: *Melanie Klein, D.W. Winnicott*
- NeoFreudian/Interpersonal: *Alfred Adler, Karen Horney, Carl Jung, Harry S Sullivan*
- Humanism/Existentialism: *Gordon Allport, Abraham Maslow, Rollo May, Carl Rogers*
- Radical Behaviorisms: *John B Watson, B.F. Skinner*
- Social Cognitive Theory: *Albert Bandura*
- Biological Basis of Personality: *Hans Eysenck*
- Evolutionary Psychology: *Edward O. Wilson*
- Rational Emotive Behavioral Therapy: *Albert Ellis* (This is one additional name regarded as important in the field but was not listed in *Beneath the Mask)*

There are clearly separate and sometimes conflicting theories in the field. Let us examine some of the "theories" advanced by the most important of these theorists[49]. Freud, Jung, Adler, Skinner, Ellis, Bandura and Maslow are excellent candidates for that list. Let us look at what they have to say.

First question: *Do any of these theorists provide us with a "scientifically defensible models or views of human behavior"?* Apparently not. What they do provide is therapeutic approaches to problems.

Beneath the Mask informs us that these theorists have expressed *"theories that have led to the development*

[49] Of course the answer as to which are the most important of these theorists would depend somewhat on the person being asked.

of therapeutic approaches and to an emphasis on one or another of many important factors important in the experience of human beings".

Beneath the Mask does not even list "theories" attributable to particular theorists. It only lists what it defines as *"Resultant ideas"* that each theorist has produced. Here are a few of those 'resultant ideas' attributed by *Beneath the Mask* to each of the theorist I have chosen in the particular category they have been assigned by the profession.

- Classical Psychoanalysis: *Freud*. Oedipus complex: Child parent sexual and aggressive attachments and conflicts; the mind is divided into the id, the ego and the superego. The superego represents internalized parental standards, ideals and prohibitions.
- Neo-Freudian/Interpersonal: *Jung:* Introversion-extroversion, and anima-animus as fundamental human dualism. Self actualization: healing properties of the whole self. Interpersonal definition of personality. Collective unconscious.
- Neo-Freudian/Interpersonal: *Adler*: Superiority strivings. Organ inferiority. Safeguarding mechanisms. "Gemeneinschaftgefihl" meaning "fellow feeling".
- Radical Behaviorism: *Skinner*: Semiradical behaviorism, Mind and feelings are irrelevant to understanding psychological causes. Semiradical determinism.
- Rational Emotive Behavioral Therapy: *Albert Ellis:* Developed Rational Emotive Behavior Therapy (REBT) a brief, direct, and solution-oriented therapy which focuses on resolving specific problems facing a troubled individual.

- Social Cognitive Theory: *Bandura*: The development of research and psychological theories emphasizing individual effort, self efficacy, and resilient agency
- Humanism/Existentialism: *Maslow:* Dominance feeling in monkeys. Self actualized people. Hierarchy of needs, a pyramid like structure rising form the base of physiological needs, safety needs, belonging needs, esteem needs, to the apex of s/elf actualization.

It seems that each of these men was working on a theory designed to achieve some therapeutic goal intended to help their patients. None articulate a general theory that addresses all human behavior. Moreover the disagreements between the theorists sometimes run deep. For example many theorists appear to believe psychological causes originate in the mind and feelings, while Skinner dismisses these factors as irrelevant.

APPENDIX II

Overview Of The Author's Research

This appendix is intended as a formal presentation of the reasons that prompted the writing of this book.

Psychology is defined by the American Heritage Dictionary as *The science that deals with mental processes and behavior.* Science is defined as *"knowledge attained through study and practice".*

The scientific method involves the following steps: 1. Ask a Question; 2. Do background research; 3. Construct a hypothesis; 4. Test your hypothesis by doing an experiment; 5. Analyze your data and draw a conclusion; 6. Communicate your results.

I will take the reader along the road of my research and conclusions. Phase One of the scientific process was to find out **if any single factor could be identified as the principle material cause in good relationships.**

PHASE ONE

The questions asked was: *Is there a single key factor that materially controls good relationships*?

Background research: *With the help of Dr. Irma Hoffman, a clinical psychologist, 2 years of anecdotal, informal and unscientific research was conducted.*

Construction of a hypothesis: *The hypothesis constructed is that all good relationships are a function of a single material factor, to wit the ability and desire of each person to make the other feel good about him/herself.*

Testing the hypothesis:

The following 5 minute questionnaire was designed to test the hypothesis, albeit in an anecdotal unscientific manner. Some 200 people randomly picked were asked:

Question # 1: What do you think are the key elements in good relationships?

Question # 2: Make a list of the 5 people with whom you have the best relationships.

Question # 3: Make a second list of the 5 people who make you feel the best about yourself.

Question # 4: How many people on the first list are also on the second list?

A much smaller number were also asked:

Question # 5: Make a list of the people who make you feel bad about yourself.

Question # 6: Are any of the 5 people on your best relationship list also on this last list?

Responses to the questionnaires:

Result # 1: The answers to what individuals felt were the key element or elements in a good relationship were all over the map. All the responses spoke of one or more of the 'do's, none addressed any of the don'ts. Consensus on any single or even multiple numbers of potential key elements was simply non-existent.

Result # 2: Over 90% reported that their best relationship list and their list of the people who made them feel good about themselves were ***identical***. Another 7%-9% reported that the lists were 4 out of 5 and therefore near identical.

Result # 3: Nobody reported that anybody on the list of people who make them feel bad about themselves appeared on their good relationship list.

Analyzing the data and drawing a conclusion:

Issue # 1: Conventional wisdom or what might be termed the "norm" on the question of the cause(s) or key element(s) of good relationships is not one on which all psychologists agree. There exists a cumulative list of some recommended behaviors, the compliance with which most of the time, seems to have been previously found to result in good relationships. The list consists of approximately 22 "do's", which are behaviors one should practice and some 6 "don't s", which are behaviors one should avoid. The non exhaustive list of 22 ***positive attributes*** is, in alphabetical order : Be accepting, agreeable, considerate, communicative, empathic, fair, faithful, forgiving, kind, loving, loyal, a listener, non-judgmental, reliable, respectful, responsible (both financially and otherwise), supportive, tolerant, trustworthy, trusting, and understanding.

The non exhaustive list of 6 negative attitudes to ***avoid*** is: Blaming, criticizing, condemning, ignoring, nagging and stonewalling.

The first purpose of the test was to discover whether there was any consensus among responders as to what they believed constituted one or more key elements in good relationships. There was none.

Conclusion # 1: ***No agreement existed among responders as to what the key element(s) were that caused good relationships.***

Conclusion # 2: ***Regardless of the potential accuracy of conventional wisdom on the issue, the average responder had no awareness of it.***

Issue # 2: Was there any positive correlation between the *best relationship list* and the *making me feeling good about myself list*?

The result was an extraordinary 90%-97% correlation!

Issue # 3: Was there any negative correlation between the *best relationship list* and the *making me feel bad about myself list*?

The result was an extraordinary 100%!

The Correlation is not causality conflict

At which point the intellectual conflict began between extraordinarily high statistical significance and the general concept taught to psychologists that "correlation" does not mean causality".

The occurrence of something deemed *statistically significant* is something that is unlikely to have occurred by chance. *Substantive significance* defines the importance, or meaningfulness, of a finding from a practical standpoint.

Statistical causality in law

One of the best places to examine society's attitudes towards statistical significance is to study that concept in law. In a court of law, matters of life and death are determined by "reasonable doubt". Reasonable doubt is determined by the "probability" that a particular event could have occurred by chance. Whether or not it could be a "chance" occurrence is a matter of statistical significance. The same is true in a court of law on issues of discrimination in employment practices.

Generally a thing is deemed a possible chance occurrence if it could have occurred once in 20 times, but not more often. Once in 20 times is a 5% probability. In matters of criminal trials there is no number given but the words "reasonable doubt" have been seen to mean about 95% certain, not 100%. That means that a person could be condemned to death if the court deems that the occurrence that brought the accused to trial could not have 'normally' occurred by chance more than once in 20 times.

Statistical significance begins at occurrences that rise to over one in twenty, or over 5% of the time. Results here rose to an amazing 97%. The statistical evidence is strong enough to trump the 'correlation is not causality' caveat, *at least to the point where that concept should be further explored.*

Conclusion # 3: ***All the evidence supports the single conclusion that the key element in good relationships is the ability of two people to make each other feel good about themselves.***

Further evidence

There is further ancillary evidence supporting these conclusions. First, is the scientific principle known as "Occam's razor" which states that when there is more than one possible explanation for any scientific fact, the simpler explanation is the most likely. The explanation offered here is by far the simplest extant, since it proffers a single cause as opposed to multiple causes, as the key element in all good relationships.

Second, the multiplicity of possible elements currently offered as causes renders impossible any dispositive scientific analysis. Each element constitutes a potential variable. Scientific testing cannot be done if more than one variable is being tested. Therefore one cannot hope to test for positive and negative elements cumulatively totaling anywhere from 22 to 27, in 'currently accepted psychology'.

Third is the 'probabilistic and seldom deterministic' nature of psychology. In a world of "probabilities" it seems right and proper that statistical evidence shown to be substantive be recognized as a major step forward, whether or not such evidence turns out to be absolutely dispositive in the long run.

Fourth, since it is generally agreed that "proving" any theory requires decades of practice, *it is impossible, in the short run, to ever "prove" anything.* One has to go forward on the basis of the likelihood of success. The evidence strongly supports the conclusion that this theory presents a very high likelihood of doing so.

PHASE TWO

The next step in the process of developing what became the *Ronald Bibace Theory of Personality* as well as the *Ronald Bibace Universal Theory of Human Behavior* was examining current beliefs of all human motivation.

The idea being that if a single key factor could be seen to be the key element in good relationships, and that good relationships were correctly deemed very important to one's well being, perhaps the same key factor, to wit the desire to feel good about oneself, could be postulated as the key motivation or "need" in all human behavior (past survival, of course).

Analyzing Maslow's Hierarchy of Needs

For many professionals the psychological 'gold standard' on human needs is *Maslow's Hierarchy of Needs*. That hierarchy is a pyramid of needs that begins at the base with the strongest needs, to wit: 1. Physiological needs, and then rises to the pyramid's apex as follows: 2. Safety needs, 3. Belonging needs, 4. Esteem needs, and 5. Self actualization needs.

On the basis of the principle of Occam's razor favoring simplicity it can be said that the single word "survival" encompasses both Maslow's item 1. Physiological needs, and item 2. Safety needs.

Beyond that, all three additional needs, to wit: 3. Belonging needs, 4. Esteem needs, and 5. Self actualization needs can also be properly summarized as ***The need to feel good about oneself.***

It is very clear that the feeling of belonging, self esteem and self actualization will all result in a person ***feeling good about him/herself***! It could certainly be argued that the ***degree*** to which one will feel good about oneself will rise as one feels one belongs, acquires self esteem and then through self actualization, does well in life.

But differences in degree do not constitute differences in substance. It is therefore reasonable to state what I call the *Ronald Bibace Theory of Personality*, or conclusion # 4 to wit:

Conclusion # 4: All human motivation, beyond survival, is the desire to feel good about oneself.

PHASE THREE

The next step was to ask the question: **What happens when a person fails to feel good about him/herself?**

The same scientific method was used as before

1. *Ask a Question:* **What happens when a person fails to feel good about himself?**
2. *Do background research*: The question could not reasonably be asked of individuals. That is because part of the presumption is that the person himself may not be aware of what is occurring internally. So the answers had to come from background research.

   That research indicated that a great many people who appeared to have unhappy lives and low self esteem tended to do certain specific things, while those with happy lives and high self esteem tended not to.

What surfaced was that people who did not feel good about themselves tended to do some or all of the following: Overeat, drink too much, indulge in drugs, smoke too much, indulge in excessive and sometimes aberrant sexual activity, indulge in abusive verbal and sometimes physical behavior and occasionally even criminal behavior

3. *Construct a hypothesis*; what became obvious from the research was that the substitute behavior described above was intended to help the actor 'feel good' as opposed to 'feeling good about oneself'.

   The distinction is clear: *Feeling good about oneself* is generally the result of doing things that are healthy, approved by society and that bring long term benefits. Examples are staying fit, being honest, caring, and trustworthy, helping others, being kind, loving, financially responsible, etc.

   Feeling good is often the result of giving oneself short term physical pleasure or a sense of pleasurable power, by doing things that are disapproved by society and have deleterious long term effects on oneself and others

4. *Analyzing the data and drawing a conclusion which is Conclusion # 5*:

Conclusion # 5: When a person fails to feel good or feels bad about him/herself, he/she will tend to substitute behavior intended to make him/herself feel good, usually with bad consequences for himself and others.

<u>Conclusion # 6: It follows from conclusion # 5 that from time to time the "bad consequences" will include behavior that will be detrimental to good relationships.</u>

<u>Conclusion # 7: It also follows that each and every one of us is potentially subject to that behavior</u>

<u>PHASE FOUR</u>

There now appears to be sufficient evidence to support the following findings:

1. *All human behavior past survival is motivated by a desire to feel good about oneself.*
2. *Failure to feel good about oneself will result in action intended to make one "feel good"*
3. *Making oneself feel good about oneself causes behavior generally beneficial to oneself and others.*
4. *Making one "feel good" causes behavior that is generally detrimental to oneself and others.*
5. *Such behavior is generally destructive to good relationships and potentially exists in all of us.*

The next question becomes: **<u>What short term and long term factors are important to creating both the feeling good about oneself and the feeling bad about oneself</u>**?

<u>Short term factors affecting feeling good about oneself</u>:

1. *The background research constitutes general knowledge and other scholastic research.*
2. *Constructing a hypothesis: People feel good about themselves in the short term when they have high self esteem, receive respect, love and affection from others, and successfully do that which is in keeping with the values of the society in which they live.*

3. *Testing the hypothesis: The hypothesis was tested by personal experience and questioning others.*
4. *Analysis of the data and conclusions: All of the anecdotal data and relevant scientific material supported the hypothetical proposition.*

Long term factors of what makes a person feel good about him/herself

1. *The background research constitutes general knowledge and other scholastic research.*
2. *Constructing a hypothesis: People feel good about themselves in the long term if they have received a great deal of love, affection, emotional support and understanding in their formative years, from birth to age 18. The concept of "emotional currency", "emotional capital" and "emotional interest" was postulated.*

   "Emotional currency" is what the child receives in the form of all the positive elements mentioned above that serve to provide the child with a sense of high self worth and self esteem. The continuing receipt over years of this "currency" accumulates just like the accumulation of cash deposited in a "trust fund" for the child. The result is a store of "emotional capital".

   Moreover, just like cash interest that the trust fund child can draw for life on his "trust fund" financial capital, the "emotional capital" provides the child with "emotional interest" in the form of a feeling of self worth and self esteem that lasts a lifetime.
3. *Testing the hypothesis: The hypothesis was tested by personal experience and questioning others.*

4. *Analysis of the date and conclusions: All of the anecdotal data and relevant scientific material supported the hypothetical proposition.*

PHASE FIVE

Let us now ask the next questions

What short term and long term factors are important to creating the feeling bad about oneself?

Short term factors:

The background research constitutes general knowledge and other scholastic research.

1. *Constructing a hypothesis: People feel bad about themselves in the short term when they suffer from some or all of the following: low self esteem, consider themselves inadequate in comparison to their peers, do not receive respect, love and affection from others, and often fail to do that which is in keeping with the values of the society in which they live.*
2. *Testing the hypothesis: The hypothesis was tested by personal experience and questioning others.*
3. *Analysis of the date and conclusions: All of the anecdotal data and relevant scientific material supported the hypothetical proposition.*

Long term factors:

The background research constitutes general knowledge and other scholastic research.

1. *Constructing a hypothesis: People feel bad about themselves in the long term when they have failed to receive the critical emotional currency and emotional capital in their early years. As a result they indefinitely suffer from low self esteem and*

consider themselves inadequate in comparison to their peers. This often occurs regardless of their eventual success, however substantial.

2. *Testing the hypothesis: The hypothesis was tested by personal experience and questioning others.*
3. *Analysis of the date and conclusions: A very high level of the anecdotal data and relevant scientific material supported the hypothesis.*

PHASE SIX

There is now enough evidence to support the following findings sufficiently to pursue further research:

1. *All human behavior past survival is motivated by a desire to feel good about oneself.*
2. *Failure to feel good about oneself will result in action intended to make one "feel good"*
3. *Making oneself feel good about oneself results in behavior generally beneficial to oneself and others.*
4. *Making oneself feel good results in behavior that is generally detrimental to oneself and others.*
5. *There are short and long term reasons for both feeling good about oneself and feeling bad about oneself.*
6. *The long term reasons for either feeling good or bad about oneself are a function of how much love, affection and self esteem one felt in one's formative years.*
7. *The short term reasons for feeling good or bad about oneself are usually a function of how much one measures up to societal standards in one's behavior and achievements, as well as how much one receives immediate love, affection and self esteem support.*

Assuming the material accuracy of the foregoing we know what it takes to achieve good relationships and what may exist within oneself that may prevent one from doing what one wishes to do.

This brings us to the next question:

What degree of control can we exercise over our need to feel good about ourselves that may produce bad outcomes?

PHASE SEVEN

This brings us to the issue of the brain and its separate parts. A very limited working hypothesis sufficient for our purpose is that there are two relevant parts of the brain that affect our decision making. One part or the "me" is the *logical* "neo-cortex" referred to as the Logical Me. The other part is the *limbic* emotional brain, referred to as the Beast.

1. *The question is: What degree of control does the 'logical me' in each of us exercise over behavior?*
2. *The background research constitutes general knowledge and other scholastic anecdotal research.*
3. *Constructing a hypothesis: The hypothesis is that the degree of control over our behavior that we are able to exercise is a function of the degree of control the "beast" within us allows. That degree of control is directly related to the level of emotional capital we possess and the immediate level of stress to which we are submitted.*
4. *Testing the hypothesis: Personal introspection and the general observation that so many people refer to aberrant behavior by stating quite sincerely: I don't know how I could have said nor done that.*

Then there is the continuing saga of men and even occasionally women, who physically abuse their spouses. They return later, full of remorse and in tears sincerely vowing that they will never do it again, only to repeat the behavior again and again.

Finally the apparent virtually 100% correlation between mass murderers, serial killers and others whose crimes make absolutely no apparent sense, and the high level of their childhood traumas, support the theory that there is within all of us a 'beast' that can take over our behavior.

The level of egregiousness the "beast" within us is capable of inflicting on others appears to be directly proportional to the level of abuse and mistreatment received as a child.

Conclusion # 8. Everybody possesses a Beast within him capable of behaving in a very harmful way to himself and others.

Conclusion # 9. The level of egregiousness of the beast behavior's appears to be directly proportional to the level of abuse and mistreatment suffered in childhood.

PHASE EIGHT

That brings us to the last question: Is there any way in which we can control the "beast" within us?

Assuming the validity of all the previous analysis we can postulate the following:

Since both my "logical me" and "my beast" want the same "feeling good about themselves" and since absent that "feeling good about himself" the beast reverts to simply "feeling good" behavior, if the beast can be brought back to "feeling good about itself" in some way, there will be no further need for destructive "feel good" behavior.

That brings us to the next postulate:

1. *In all civilized societies knowledge, intelligence and wisdom is prized.*
2. *If the Beast can be made to recognize that he/she possesses superior knowledge and understanding of the human psyche, it might suffice to provide the Beast with a sufficient level of "feeling good about himself" to overcome the need to satisfy the "feel good" need otherwise present.*
3. *So if my Beast is told by my "Logical Me" (or others) that by recognizing the internal functioning of the brain and its ability to make my Beast do bad things, my Beast is demonstrating superior knowledge, that realization alone may well provide sufficient feeling good about himself to my Beast to overcome the need for the bad behavior.*

This theory was tested twice and worked remarkably well. To test it further requires that the participants understand the entire theory and accept it as valid. That will have to wait for this book to be published and enough people to understand and practice this theory to validate further testing.

Conclusion Number 10: It is likely that the Beast within us can be made to give up destructive behavior by becoming aware of the process by which it is acting, which then provides a feeling of possession of superior knowledge sufficient to create the "feeling good about itself" that negated any need for the

<u>destructive behavior triggered by the need to "feel good".</u>

APPENDIX III

<u>List Of Significant Differences With Conventional Wisdom</u>

There appear to be sufficient differences between what this book postulates and conventional wisdom to at least suggest that some progress is perceptible in the quest for understanding human behavior. Here is a list of these differences.

1. *<u>The Ronald Bibace Theory of Personality</u> and/or <u>The Ronald Bibace Universal Theory of Human Behavior</u> is the only specific theory of personality that purports to encompass motivation for all human behavior, to wit:*

   All human behavior past survival is motivated by the desire to feel good about ourselves or to avoid feeling bad about ourselves.

2. *The book postulates the only **<u>personally verifiable explanation</u>** for good relationships between people, (by the self test) to wit:*

   The key to all good relationships is the ability and desire of one person to make another feel good about him/herself.

3. *The book postulates, (as did Freud with the concept of id, ego and superego), but perhaps with more easily understandable explanations of the basic causes,* ***the existence of separate personalities*** *within each of us, to wit: The emotional, illogical wild "Beast" (Freud's id) and the logical, rational, "Logical Me". (A combination of Freud's ego and superego)*
4. *The book postulates with ample evidence, the potential under certain circumstances, for a* ***complete lack of control*** *of the Logical Me over the Beast, raising issues of the morality and appropriateness of society's particular punishments for particular acts.*

5. *The book postulates the shift by the Beast from seeking to* ***feel good about itself*** *to simply* ***feeling good****, the first act being positive and the second negative, both to itself and others.*

6. *The book postulates the explanations for the* ***differences between the power of particular different Beasts over the related Logical Me's****, how to identify and cope with those differences and the long term solutions for society.*

7. *The book postulates* ***the application of these principles to a wide range of human affairs****, among which the more important are business, and state concerns such as bullying, gangs and suicide bombers, as well as religion*

8. *The book postulates one solution by which an individual* ***may be able to overcome his/her own Beast's control over his/her Logical Me****, swiftly, effectively and permanently.*
9. ***The postulated explanations are supported in theory by the scientific principle known as Occam's Razor, according to which, among competing explanations, the simplest explanation to observed phenomena is probably the right one.***

10. *The book makes specific predictions that can be tested.*

About The Author

The author, Ronald Bibace, was born in Alexandria, Egypt in 1934 of French speaking parents. He grew up speaking French, English, Italian, and Arabic, which was a common experience for Egyptian born individuals of European ancestry. His family of Sephardic Jews was originally from Spain. The family had to leave in 1492 for North Africa because Spanish Queen Isabella decreed that all non-Catholics would have to convert to Catholicism, leave, or be killed.

Ronald attended English speaking schools in Alexandria and left for Canada in 1952 to attend the University of British Columbia, where he did two years of undergraduate work. In 1954 he moved to Montreal, to which his uncle Joseph Pardo had emigrated from Egypt, to attend McGill University. He graduated from McGill in 1956 with a Bachelor of Commerce Degree and obtained a Licentiate in Accounting in 1956. (A bachelor of Commerce degree is the equivalent of a Business Administration degree in the USA.) A Licentiate in Accounting is the requirement in Canada to become a Chartered Accountant, which he then became. (A Chartered Accountant is the Canadian equivalent of a Certified Public Accountant in the USA.)

In 1957 he started a real estate brokerage business in Montreal. In 1960 he married Joska Levy and had two children; Claudia in 1964 and Wendy in 1969. In 1962 he graduated from Concordia University in Montreal, (then called Sir George Williams University) with a Bachelor of Arts degree. In 1971 he moved his family to South Florida and continued a successful career in real estate brokerage and construction, landscaping and other business activities.

In 1995, although not a lawyer, he wrote the continuation of the Federalist Papers as a labor of love and signed it PUBLIUS II (the original Federalist papers written by Madison, Hamilton, and Jay were signed PUBLIUS). The work is available on his Web site at www.constitutionalguardian.com, addressing certain constitutional issues he deems particularly important to the welfare of the nation. That work and this book are the only two literary efforts by this writer.

DISCLAIMER

This book is written for the purpose of entertaining the reader with the experiences and insights of the author. It is not intended as a guide or substitute for whatever professional help a particular reader may need and should not be used for those ends.

With respect to whatever helpful life lessons a reader may derive from the author's experiences and ideas, I urge the reader to heed the advice of the great eastern philosopher and sage known as Buddha. "*Believe nothing, no matter where you read it, or who said it, no matter if I have said it, unless it agrees with your own reason and your own common sense.*"

I am occasionally asked for advice. I always preface my remarks as follows:

I do not believe in telling anyone what to do. Each of us must make up his own mind as to his path in life based on his own particular circumstances and values.

All I can do is tell you what I would do in certain situations in keeping with my own particular set of life circumstances and values. I can also tell you what I think the consequences of my suggested actions would be for me. I suggest that you listen to what I say. Then think about it and discuss what you heard with others you respect. Then and only if you are convinced in your own mind and as a result of your own thoughtful evaluation and assessment, that certain suggestions would be right for you, should you make them a part of your own thinking and behavior.

Ronald Bibace – March 4, 2010

Breinigsville, PA USA
10 February 2011

255332BV00001B/65/P